GIRLFAG

A LIFE TOLD IN SEX AND MUSICALS

Janet W. Hardy

Beyond
Binary
Books

Published in the United States by Beyond Binary Books, Eugene, OR, *www.beyondbinarybooks.com*. Distributed by SCB Distributors, Gardena, CA.

TABLE OF CONTENTS

PERMISSIONS

ACKNOWLEDGMENTS

Of tremendous help in the preparation of this book:

My fabulous and infinitely patient thesis advisors, Marilyn Abild-skov and Russ Rymer, who I now dub Honorary Queers...

My colleagues and teachers in the MFA program and the English Department at St. Mary's College, especially David DeRose, Wesley Gibson, Rosemary Graham, Barry Horwitz, Vicki Hudson, Erich Miller and Jason Sattler...

My sons, Miles and Ben Taber, and my former husband Frank Taber...

My late mother, my father and their wonderful spouses...

The *Girlfag* readers' list...

The wonderful folks at Kickstarter who helped raise the money to make this book a reality, especially Craig L Louis...

Amy (RIP), Kay and Bo, who pried me away from my desk when I needed it...

Special thanks to Jill Nagel for coining the word "girlfag" and thus instantly crystallizing a lifetime of thoughts and yearnings...

And a grateful shout-out to an uncountable assortment of perverts, fags, dykes, fencesitters, trannies, drag queens, tantrikas and sex magick practitioners, who helped make me (for good or ill) what I am today, and who made this book possible.

Out of respect for the choices of some of the people I have portrayed in this book, I have changed their names and disguised key details about their lives. Others appear under their real names and descriptions, but are, as all authors' subjects must be, susceptible to a biased and erratic memory. If I got anything wrong, my friends, I'm sorry.

"I'M TELLING YOU, THE ONLY TIMES I FEEL I'M IN THE PRESENCE OF GOD ARE WHEN I'M HAVING SEX, AND DURING A GREAT BROADWAY MUSICAL."

— Father Dan, in Paul Rudnick's *Jeffrey* (1995)

This book is dedicated to
Paul (the one who's still alive), who helped me think it...
Dossie, who helped me feel it...
and Edward, who helps me live it.

FOREWORD
BY CAROL QUEEN & ROBERT LAWRENCE

CAROL: I talked to a videographer from Brazil today about queer language. I was, perhaps, a good person to discuss this because, one, I have lived so fucking long by now that I remember when words meant different things than they do today, and two, because I have myself embraced most of the sexual identities known to woman, man, and all those in between. I believe this might be why Janet reached out to me to contribute this foreword: because I know them when I see them.

So, queer. It began as an epithet... well, before that, as something else, a word meaning to describe that which was, variously, twisty or weird or wise. Later, as we know, it became a word we took back; at least, some of us did. Then it became the sexual identity of a generation, which has no fixed definition beyond "non-heteronormative," or, maybe, "I'm basically open to anything."

("Oh, Johnny! You're such a rebel! What are you rebelling against?"
"Whattaya got?")
And then, fag.

Before it was an epithet, before a cigarette, it was a stick of wood, they tell us: a faggot which could fuel a flame foul enough to burn a witch. But most of us have things in mind far distant from the *Malleus Mallificarum* when we contemplate this term. We might not like it — it may trigger in us the taunts of schoolyard enemies, or we may be old enough to think about, say, the dubious but of-its-moment sociology of *The Boys in the Band.* Or we may understand it more neutrally — no, wait, this is never really a neutral word; it might evoke splendid images of Radical Faeries, Cole Porter or Oscar Wilde brilliance, or my favorite link, the men of my youth who gathered together as Faggots Against Fascism.

But the people who don't like it... to them, it's always hate speech. Its own twisty history contains so much opprobrium, and "fag" as epithet begins being hurled when we are so vulnerably young, that to some of us, it has never been on the agenda to rehabilitate. If the "It Gets Better" Project is right, perhaps these men are thinking, we will manage to scrub the word out of everyone's consciousness, along with the "What kind of a queer-ass, nellie weirdo are *you?*" undertone it has always, to them, seemed to carry.

But listen: The way its queer proponents use "fag," it is a deeply useful word without a close synonym. It tends to telegraph that the man in question is not butch, and may indeed be quite fey. (The deep-in-closet men of my mother's day might have been called "sweet" instead, at least by people who were being nice.) Fag implies head-held-high rebellion in the same way that queer does: You may try to use this word against me, but I'll cloak myself in it with pride, and it'll repel all your sticks and stones and insults. Like a certain N-word, often used as hate language, when it is reappropriated it becomes an IN word, used to separate friend from foe, used to solidify bonds of community and cultural like-mindedness. For that matter, slut (whether or not the Slut is Walking) has been used the same way. It's telling, I think, that all these slangy, it's-ours-now-we-took-it-back terms are controversial and never really proper speech both within and outside of the communities they reference: homosexuals, African-Americans, and women may embrace them or find them hurtful, hateful, and offensive, and this demonstrates to us that these identities, much less the underground nomenclatures associated with them, are not monolithic and singular, emotionally or culturally.

What word, therefore, given this on-the-hoof definition, would fag-deniers like us to use instead? "Gay man"? It doesn't automatically bring the fey; it's too general. Today there are so many variants on the gay male model that it does not paint the sort of picture that "fag" begins to do. It has little specificity. "Homosexual"? Too retro! And also not sufficiently specific. Even if people in the old days of "homo" and "homosexual" believed that gay men were by definition effeminate—which only meant that a) they were too ignorant to possess finely tuned gaydar and b) they were too straight to figure out where the *really* interesting gay bars were — they were always wrong: after all, Walt Whitman used to fall in love with trade every time he got on the trolley.

Maybe "queen" comes closest, but honey, that's *mine.* Not only that, it's so closely associated with its related term "drag queen" that it retains a touch of specificity in defining a non-butch queer man that "fag" does not. Plus, in real-life usage, "queen" is a sort of all-purpose queer suffix: not just "drag queen," but also "drama queen," "rice queen," "leather queen," and so many more iterations of personality and desire can be packed into the baggage this word carries. As such, it's as indispensable as "fag," but not exactly a synonym.

And if Janet had called her book "Girlqueen," you would not have received the etymological message that she wishes to introduce before you even picked the book up at a bookstore (provided there remain any of those ancient institutions where you are, and provided you are reading a tree-derived item and not something made out of bits, bytes, light, and plastic): "Queen" is a female-coded term, whereas "fag" (lately) isn't. "Girlfag" works as the opening line of a flirtation, a conversation, a manifesto, or a memoir because, in our binary culture, it's guaranteed to make everyone but the other girlfags themselves go "Huh?" And this, perhaps, opens the door to wonder: How can a girl be a fag? How can a woman identify herself so far outside the borders of what a woman is told, in this opposite-sexed culture, she can be? Some people will want to know more.

To which I have no clarification to make; curious ones, Janet will explain. Wait – first, let's let Robert tell you more about it.

ROBERT: Girlfags are quixotically both more and less masculine [than boyfags]. Cis-ter or otherwise, their knowledge and bitchy loving support for the human condition provides acceptance in any milieu. I love the quick-witted loving sauciness of girlfags. They own the space they are in with the fresh-faced gentle-mindedness of Whitman, while having the promise of a special place in their heart to care for the fragile thing I am as a male. Easily not mistaken as fag hags, they confidently wander open-faced into places where they should be unwelcome yet find space, stand fast and are admired. I envy girlfags; as a fey male I regularly face the butch shun from The Gay because of my challenging long hair, soft voice and quick wrist. But with a girlfag standing next to me I am safe from the opprobrium of the male-only folk and having one next to me allows for a second pair of eyes to look and see if anyone is interesting or interested. We can team them and they never know how it all happened so fast.

I was told a while back by a local sex club owner that bringing a girlfag into a sex club would be insulting to men – so I did. That girlfag is now the only cis-female to be an honorary member of The Trough, a men-only piss club here in San Francisco. She impressed the club folk there so much, they adopted that girlfag in and changed history. In fact we went to the Blow Buddies the very next week.

When did girlfags come to the fore in my life? As the HIV plague hit, it was they who held onto the fag traditions while people were so very busy dying. It was the girlfags who held us and washed us, fed us as we all screamed not so quietly while our creative and very-much-unwilling-to-be-assimilated people disappeared back into the earth. They knew that if we ran out of men, someone had to hold the faggot tradition, so they stepped in to cover the need for holding love, beauty and creativity while being able to laughingly flay your skin with one bitchy word. Oddly, looking back, they'd been there all along, but we were too busy being us to notice.

CAROL: I lied. I *do* have something to say about the liminal identity of the girlfag: I am one myself.

In certain circles I am best known for my book *The Leather Daddy and the Femme,* in which a crossdressing woman named Miranda (Randy, when she's in drag) falls for a gay leatherman named Jack Prosper. This book is not, as many have assumed, my autobiography, except insofar as the deepest fantasy shows the way to one's truest desires, the person that lives inside the person we cook up to live our public lives for us. I'm not much of a crossdresser, at least I wasn't then (I didn't look old enough to go to the bathhouses I'd have wanted to sneak into). But the men I love most have always been fags. Not all gay men are fags, and not all bisexual men are either; it takes a special guy to both embody Big Faggitude and also want to square his shoulders and stay in the same room with hot pussy. But a few good men have made that space for me, and for themselves.

I complicated this by identifying as a dyke for many years, and parenthetically, I'd like to offer the Facebook Generation the insight that "It's Complicated" is a great sexual identity as well as relationship status. Ooops! Digressed. Where was I? Oh, yes: *Dyke* – another hate word that has been very successfully reclaimed! But in my case, saying I was a dyke was only true insofar as "dyke" is an identity that can in-corporate both a fierce love of, and identification with, women – plus in my case, a fierce love of, and identification with, fags. There really is no actual word for the thing that I was. But that is so true of so many of us: it's the reason we now just say "queer."

For a minute, after a youth full of bedpost-notching, the kind of frisky experimental fucking that teenagers do best, I tried to stay stable and lesbian — well, that was never going to take, but I subsumed my desire for male bodies, my delight at sparring with men as a prelude to fucking them, into erotically charged friendships with gay men. One after the other, I created gay activist events and groups, my love for my co-conspirators floating like oil on top of the water that was my connection with my women lovers. I might have gone on forever this way, my girlfaggy bisexuality (and of course, a girlfag is a variety of bisexual, whether or not she embraces that larger term) living mostly in frantic masturbation sessions fueled by gay porn.

Until James Campbell, a gay man who should have pretended not to notice my crush, instead kissed me goodnight until the windows of his Volkswagen steamed. Until this one safely unattainable man turned out to be polymorphous enough — or enough in love with me too — to allow acknowledged, not silenced, erotic feeling to float in the air between us. And how could a queer activist not take seriously the challenge and dilemma of forbidden love? We would never have wanted to be seen as any kind of straight, but the freedom to love is what our whole struggle was about. AIDS was the reason I went from lesbian to bisexual: that I might lose James made me see that the heart of my turn-on was pure love.

James opened the door to everything: queer men, queer sex, a newly (re)embraced bisexual identity, San Francisco — because of course once I'd become that weird a dyke in my small university city, I had to get out of Dodge and head to the only place that would have me — which, in turn, let me grow into the person I have become. (Visiting San Francisco with my girlfriend Ellen during Pride Week in 1979, we walked the block from Market to 18th Street after the march, and it was so thick with men, bare-chested, Izod-shirted, tight-Levi'd, chaps-assed, nipple-ringed, drunk on Gay Pride and brotherhood, that we had to cling to each other's hands like swimmers fighting rapids to avoid being split apart and losing one another. It was the first time I had ever been surrounded by men with no feeling at all of fear. We were pressed in like a scrum of sardines, we were held securely between sweaty men, and I was so happy, I have no idea how I mustered the strength the next day to leave the city and go back to the mundane world where dykes played softball and argued about whether it was male-identified to read *On Our Backs*. San Francisco was New Jerusalem, as my fag friend Will called it — it was Oz.)

James wrote me a letter of recommendation when I applied to be the first woman working at an AIDS service organization — I didn't get the job, because it was still too soon for women to really be part of the change that would change everything, but James said this: "Carol is more comfortable with and for gay men than most gay men I know."

That's not the definition of girlfaggitude — it leaves out the erotic charge — but it is central, I think, to the POV of a girlfag to understand fags as a superior kind of man, nay, human, and to live that belief.

James did not live to read *The Leather Daddy and the Femme,* to watch *Bend Over Boyfriend,* to realize that I *did* walk through the door he opened. Robert's right, I think, that some of us female-bodied and faggot-souled folk had to step up to help live lives that threatened to go extinct. Many men since then, especially Robert, have offered me the opportunity to explore pomosexual pleasures, the space between gay and straight and male and female that allows the people who occupy it to construct their humanness with any building blocks of gender identity, personality, and sexual desire and play that fit the life they want to build.

But this isn't the time for my story, really. Janet will show you how it's done — you'll see. Read on.

OVERTURE

I am two months shy of my sixth birthday, and I have been promised a special Christmastime treat: tonight I will be allowed to stay up late to watch *Peter Pan* on TV.

In honor of the occasion we eat dinner in the den: grilled cheese sandwiches, tomato soup in mugs. My sister, still in diapers, is already in bed. I sit in front of the black-and-white TV in my best nightie, knees drawn up to chest so my feet stay warm inside the flannel, arms wrapped around my legs. My hair, released from its two tight daytime braids, falls in waves down my back.

Peter's fists are on his hips. His legs are spread wide. He leans backward and crows like a rooster, *Er-er-er-er-ERRR!!* And then his feet leave the floor, as though gravity never existed, and he flies, over the city, through the bright stars, brave and beautiful in the cold night air. I am flying with him, wide-eyed and breathless, leaving my body behind on the suburban carpet, parents half-remembered on the couch behind me, sandwich cooling on the melamine plate by my side.

We are in Neverland. I have learned to placate fairies and to avoid mermaids. Peter has built me a house — no, wait, he built the house for Wendy.

We hear grownup male voices coming toward us, jovial and threatening. Pirates.

We're bloody buccaneers — HUH!
And each a murderous crook — HUH!
We massacre Indians, kill little boys,
and take them to Captain Hook!
Yo-ho, yo-ho, the terrible Captain Hook!

Captain Hook has long black ringlets and a velvet coat with gold on it and deep lace cuffs that almost hide his glittering sharp hook. I am mesmerized by his mouth, the way his lips move with each exquisite word. His eyebrows rise and flutter and so do his hands. His tall boots have silver buckles on them and he takes tiny steps like a dancer.

Captain Hook is sad: *No little children love me,* he mourns. I am a little child and I love Captain Hook, I love him so much. I want to punish him for all the bad things he has done — no, wait, I want Peter to do that. I want Peter to hold him while he cries, to feel pirate tears on his shoulder. I want to live in Neverland with Peter and Wendy and Captain Hook. I want tall boots with silver buckles. I want a little house where I can tell stories. I want to fly.

I

TALL BOOTS WITH SILVER BUCKLES

This is a book about dissolution, in all the senses of the word. Lawyers call a divorce a "dissolution," and there's a divorce in here, although a rather anticlimactic one. And some people say you're "dissolute" if they think that you're morally not quite up to par, and, well, there's a lot of that in here too, mostly with me at its center.

But "dissolution" is the noun form of the verb "dissolve." Moviemakers use a "dissolve" to transition from one scene to the next, so that they can jump all around their story, sometimes to things that seem irrelevant at the time but that start to make more sense as the movie progresses. And physicists mean "dissolve" to mean the softening of edges, the loss of boundaries, the point where the lump of sugar becomes smaller and smaller, and then the sugar is liquid, and then the water is sweet.

And that's really what this book is about: dissolving, dissolution, solution. Edges softening, edges disappearing, edges so far gone that you realize they never existed and that you're standing like Wile E Coyote in midair. Don't worry, you'll only fall if you think too much about how you got there in the first place.

*A*t this point it seems as though I should introduce myself. But given that I'm no longer confident of the edges of most words, I'm not quite sure how to. Let's just say that the occasional stranger who, registering my closely barbered hair and deep speaking voice, addresses me as "sir," probably has not observed the size of my rear end.

At the time most of this book was written, I was living in Oakland, California, home to throngs of San Francisco refugees driven out of the city by upward-zooming rent or downward-pressing fog. (I now live in Eugene, Oregon, which is where Californians go when they can't hack California any more.) Oakland has the highest lesbian population and the third-highest gay population of any major city in the U.S. Whatever that means, I felt utterly at home there. There, when I mentioned my spouse, people asked how long she and I had been together. I rarely corrected them; they had the right idea even if the facts weren't quite accurate.

I have raised two sons. I run a small business that has careened wildly, as such enterprises will do, from terrifying failure to temporarily reassuring success and back again, several times. I am a sadomasochist. I am currently in my third and fourth long-term relationships. I am not yet a grandmother but I bake like one. I listen to a lot of show tunes.

You may now feel that you understand me less than you did before you began this introduction. That happens a lot when I try to explain myself.

I have always wanted in.

In: to the twisty humor and campy adulation.

In: to the why-not sex and effortless fabulosity.

In: to the lost-soul neediness, the fuck-you self-definition, the endless streams of gossip and in-jokes and flirtation and sheer raw Eros.

I recognized it long before I understood it. Even as a child I responded to vague cultural referents and deeply coded television characters, recognizing my place in a world that danced just beyond the reach of my ineluctably female fingertips.

The other girls all had crushes on some Beatle, or perhaps David Cassidy or Bobby Sherman or a Monkee or, for the bad girls, a Rolling Stone. Here's who I had crushes on: Cyril Ritchard as Captain Hook in *Peter Pan;* Jonathan Harris as Dr. Smith on *Lost In Space;* Roddy McDowall as the Bookworm on *Batman;* Charles Nelson Reilly as the captain's nephew on *The Ghost and Mrs. Muir;* Vincent Price as everything, in everything.

If you look up the biographies of the men I had crushes on, you may be surprised. Harris was married to the same woman for sixty-four years. McDowall's homosexuality was one of Hollywood's worst-kept secrets. Price was married to three different women, the first for ten years, the second for twenty-four years, the third for seventeen years until her death. Reilly anticlimactically came out at the age of 69.

You never can tell.

*P*aul kneels above me, his slim form in a halo of moonlight. His long curls tumble over his creamy, narrow shoulders. His erection is long and slender, although I don't know that because it's the first one I've ever seen. It is soft to touch but firm to grasp. He can move it by tensing and relaxing his tummy muscles, which makes me giggle.

If Paul could read this, he'd be hugely amused to be remembered this way. And it's not like I don't have a lot of other memories of him; it's just that this is the one I like best.

But since this part is a story and should be told in order, I'll start at the beginning. Honors Freshman English, 1969, Palos Verdes, California. Someone says something, someone else laughs, the next day a note gets passed, some other time we sit together at lunch, and then we're boyfriend and girlfriend. I'm pale and stocky, a recent East Coast transplant with an outsized vocabulary, and I ostentatiously write poetry in teensy vertical script in the margins of my notebooks. He's small, puppyish, not quite clear of puberty, with a curvy mouth and a spray of freckles and hair longer than most boys our age dared wear it back then.

We rarely touched one another. I know we didn't kiss because I remember my first kiss and it was with someone else several years later. My best friend Candi said she'd already kissed him, but I was afraid to ask him if that was true or not.

I remember going over to his place one day, lying to my parents, telling them his mother was going to be there, but she wasn't. I'm pretty sure she left us alone there on purpose. He cooked for me – as the only child of a divorced mother he'd learned to cook, and he sautéed some spinach, and taught me to sprinkle it with vinegar, which I'd never had before but is the way I still eat spinach now. We chased each other around the apartment and played tickle games. We lay together on a couch and talked about what it felt like to lie right up next to another warm body. I interpreted the feelings in my pelvis as needing to pee, and kept having to get up and go to the bathroom.

One day soon afterward we were talking to Connie, the only cheerleader who was also in Honors English. Connie had long blond hair and innocent blue eyes; she seemed like the sort of girl who ought to dot her i's with little hearts, or at least circles, but she didn't. She also seemed like the sort of girl who didn't talk to people like Paul and me, but she was actually very nice.

"Wow, where'd you get those bruises on your arms?" I asked her.

"Oh, you know – Bill and I went to the drive-in Saturday night, and I spent all night fighting him off," she said, avoiding my eyes and Paul's too. "You know what boys are." A lot of girls would have sounded a little bit proud when they said something like that, especially since Bill was that year's star quarterback, but Connie didn't; she sounded sad and tired and a little scared. Paul and I never talked about this conversation again: if that was what boys were and what girls were, then what were *we?*

Nevertheless, soon afterward I decided I had to go to the Soph Doll Dance: I think I wanted to prove that I could go if I wanted to. Paul wasn't thrilled with the idea, but I pleaded until he gave in.

That was soon after Zeffirelli's *Romeo and Juliet* and the girls were all wearing empire waists and scoop necks, and so was I, in royal-blue velvet. Connie, in yellow satin, was crowned Soph Doll. Paul wanted to wear his Sergeant Pepper-style gold-trimmed bandleader's jacket, but his mother made him wear a tux.

Instead of a corsage he gave me a homemade beanbag: a little fox, made of scraps of felt, that he'd run up on his mother's sewing machine. He wasn't much of a seamstress and all the beans soon leaked out and made a big mess in my bedroom. Now I wish I'd kept the felt skin.

We danced to the slow numbers. We were exactly the same height and his cheek was soft and nearly beardless against mine.

A month or two later we were talking on the phone. I remember twisting the long black umbilical phone cord around and around my finger as we talked.

"I have to tell you something," he said. "I'm gay." I was the first person he told. Soon afterward he told everybody. If he got beat up or humiliated because of it, he never said so.

So I got another boyfriend. Alec didn't touch me much either, although he did eventually get around to kissing me, in a rather tentative and bruise-free way. His mother often left us alone together. (I think these mothers imputed to me a magical gay-boy-converting ability that was totally out of proportion to my charms, then or now.)

Paul's mother made him go spend the summer with his uncle, a minister, in Waco, Texas. I tried to write a poem about it but my imagination faltered at the idea of beautiful, fey little Paul in barren Waco.

Before he left, he signed my yearbook. As I look at it now, Paul's handwriting is chaotic, vertical in one sentence, almost illegibly slanted in the next, and it wanders all over the page. He's written, "We had a really good year together, even though you hated me at the beginning of the year." I don't remember that. I guess I must have gotten mad at him about the being-gay thing. I know that by the end of the year we were still spending a lot of time together.

In the yearbook, Paul also wrote, "Please come to my housewarming party," and I do remember that. As soon as school was over Paul moved in with his lover and his lover's wife, into a tired-looking ranch house in the Silver Lake district. Five or six of us rode down together to the party, in someone's father's enormous beige station wagon that we'd borrowed because we didn't all fit into Candi's Beetle.

We were younger than anyone else there except Paul. Everyone else except the lover's wife was gay. We sat on the floor and passed a bottle of wine and a joint. The lover's wife, who wore her hair in a single long graying braid, kept putting out trays of food, and didn't talk to us.

Candi made me guess what she was thinking. "Five words," she said. I guessed for a while and then got part of it: "You're in love with someone." "Right!" she crowed. But it was a long time before I guessed the last part: "Me?"

We lay, drunk and dizzy, on the floor, and necked for hours, but I wouldn't let her unzip my leotard.

*L*ater that summer Paul invited me to visit him and his new lover, EJ — I don't know what became of the one with the wife. EJ was a lot older than Paul or me, but since I was seventeen and Paul was sixteen that wasn't too surprising. We spent the whole afternoon on EJ's bed. Paul lay on his back between EJ and me, his head on EJ's shoulder, my head on Paul's chest. EJ murmured into Paul's ear, so softly that I could barely hear it. He asked Paul about men, about being a man, about wanting men. His voice was gentle and insinuating and each question led with inexorable logic to the next. It went on for hours. None of Paul's answers were right and EJ's questions got more pointed, nastier. Paul writhed and cried and there was nothing I could do about it. He was being punished because of me and I couldn't help him. I put my hand on EJ's arm but he ignored me. "You're not really gay," EJ cooed. "You're just playing around with this. Come back when you're serious." Paul cried harder. I put my hand on his heart and felt it hammering but I was invisible and I couldn't slow it down. The tension was building in his muscles and I thought he might be about to leap up and run away from us. And then EJ stopped, and told him he was a good boy, and of *course* he was gay,

and held him while he sobbed, and I patted him on
the back and wiped away a tear or two when I could
reach his face.

The pornographer and sexual philosopher Marco Vassi wrote, "Sex is, as the traditionalists have it, a vehicle for making babies, and nothing else.... However, there is a vast realm of erotic behavior which falls outside this stricture, and for that I have designated the term *metasex*."

He adds, "As against my massive involvement in metasexual activity, my experience of sex has been limited." Mine too, on both counts. By Vassi's definition, I've only had sex — which "involves a male and a female, penetration by penis into vagina, and ejaculation at the period of fertility" — twice in my life: that's how long it took my first husband and me to conceive our second son, the one we had on purpose. I've had almost every kind of metasex you can imagine.

Here's the thing: Once you wrap your brain around the idea of metasex, it gets kind of hard to tell when you're having it and when you're not.

Not too long after the EJ afternoon, I decided I needed to have intercourse, maybe to prove that I could if I wanted to. Alec had kissed me a few times and touched my breasts once, and there was the afternoon with Candi, and that was about it for my sexual experience. I was on The Pill, though, because my mother had asked if I wanted it and I'd told her yes.

Alec was off being a camp counselor for the summer. Paul was the one I asked. He thought about it for a moment, grinned, and said, "Cool!"

We waited till my house was empty. We used the fold-out sofa in the guest room because my room only had single beds.

We tried and tried. His erection was rubbery and unreliable. It seemed impossible that anything would ever get into my tiny hole. We'd try, and he'd bend, and I'd yelp in pain, and he'd wilt, and we'd cuddle for a while and touch each other and giggle, and then we'd try again.

Finally it was dawn and we still hadn't fucked. We were sweetly sore, and sleepy. We dozed for a while and then got dressed and hugged and he went home, and the summer ended soon after.

here are many things I wish I'd known back then. Here's one of them: I am not what you'd call a passionate person. Horny, yes, often for rather extreme forms of gratification, but that's different. Horny is no harder to take care of than hungry, which sounds similar and is.

What I mean by that is that I'm not the sort of person who stalks, or attempts suicide, or dumps my spouse and kids to run away to Rio with my yoga instructor. I rarely lose my temper. I have never met a person I can't live without and I doubt I ever will. I like three cups of strong coffee with cream every morning, a down comforter on my bed, a well-stocked kitchen, and the warmth of another body against my back when I go to sleep. I hate discomfort and conflict and unhappiness.

And another: There are a few ways in which I need to be loved, but there are a lot more ways in which I don't.

*I*n the record-setting cold snap of November 1972, I was a freshman at the University of California at Santa Cruz, and Paul was at UC Santa Barbara, three hundred miles away.

UCSC at that time was past its first idealistic glories, but it was still the most radical school in the University of California system; the students called it Uncle Charlie's Summer Camp, and the locals called it the University of Communists, Socialists and Crazies. Tucked back in foggy redwoods, its widely spaced buildings were angular constructions of distressed concrete, tall glass, raw wood. It was divided up into colleges — Crown, Cowell, Merrill, Stevenson, several others — each with its own area of study; the newer colleges were called by number until a donor purchased naming rights.

My roommate, blonde and sunny and bewildered, packed up her stuffed animals and hot rollers and moved out after our fundamental incompatibility became obvious: some guy who needed crash space had come to our door one night, and he seemed nice enough, so we let him sleep in our room. Since there were only two beds, she stayed over with her friend next door. But when she came back the next morning, she found the two of us curled up together in my bunk. An empty bottle of wine, which he'd purchased in a vain attempt to loosen up my recalcitrant hymen, lay on the floor next to us. Although technically, in the language of the time, "nothing had happened," she decided she'd be happier next door permanently.

With her gone, days went by in which I spoke to nobody, and there was nothing to stop my piles of unwashed clothing, crumpled-up poems and unread textbooks from filling the room like the snow that was making its unprecedented appearance against the edges of the campus pathways.

The walk from my room in Crown to most of my classes at College Five took a brisk fifteen minutes or a meandering twenty, usually through icy fog, and I could rarely face it. Santa Cruz didn't have grades and there was no such thing as failing, so I simply didn't pass: logic, anthropology, history… anything that started before noon, or that required research, or that involved any activity besides drawing pictures and writing first drafts.

I lay awake at night humming the soundtrack to *Jesus Christ Superstar* in rhythm with my little electric alarm clock, whose fake pendulum swung in 5/4 time, then slept through the actual alarm and all my morning classes. I wrote dozens of poems, presented them in my creative writing workshops, ignored everyone's suggestions, and stashed the intact, dreadful drafts carefully away in a file box that was the only tidy item in my room.

I tried to paint a cheery mural on my closet door, something with a rainbow in it, using cheap poster paint from the supermarket. The paint sagged and ran. I soaked a towel in water over and over again and wiped it all off, then sneaked the muddy towel into the communal bathroom sink to be someone else's problem.

I cut my hair ultra-short, grew it, cut it again, bleached it, braided it to mute its brassy glow, but nothing worked; I didn't even know what "working" would look like.

I got a couple of letters from Paul, scrawled in ballpoint on typing paper, nearly illegible, the lines dropping precipitously downward as they approached the right margin. He was lonely and unhappy, but then, so was I. I wrote back when I thought about it. The letters slowed and then stopped.

I must have been cutting class the day they told us about George Sand.

Born Aurore Dupin, product of a hasty marriage between a nobleman and a birdseller's daughter, George developed a preference for men's clothing in her teens, when a family friend, a local doctor, began taking her on his daily rounds. Nobody else, the doctor argued, had as steady a hand with an amputation or as gentle a way with a sick child, and trousers were simply easier for riding and working. George found that trousers also gave you adventures that a skirt simply couldn't: people offered to sell you houses, women offered to sleep with you. But trousers wouldn't get you married to Casimir Dudevant, illegitimate son of a baron, so when she turned eighteen the trousers had to go.

She and Dudevant had a baby, then another. She did her best to be a good wife and mother. She spoiled her kids devotedly – ruining the kids but not filling her heart. On vacation at a spa, the children still toddlers, George fell passionately in love with a young magistrate. Ecstatically she proposed a *ménage à trois* to her appalled husband...

George's story would fill many books, and has. Fearless and tireless, she cherry-picked the best that 19th-century France had to offer both men and women. Her unmistakable heavy-lidded dark eyes, which look weirdly like mine, stare out of editorial cartoons, portraits by the era's finest artists, and, later, posters for the revolution of which she was a champion. In most of these, she's back in her trousers.

Dudevant divorced her after her third or fourth scandal. With her next great love Alfred de Musset, George was an avid sadomasochist (like me!), writing with glee of the bruises and bite marks on her flesh. The first time they met in private, de Musset entered George's drawing room to find her smoking a long pipe, wearing a dressing gown and embroidered Turkish slippers; he fell to his knees to caress the delicate embroidery. Their stormy affair lasted several years: he called her "the most womanly woman."

Next came Frédéric Chopin, with whom she was the tenderest of fag-hags (like me!). She was infatuated with Chopin's fey fragile beauty and prodigious talent, but he found her unfeminine and was terrified of her obvious carnality. George finally bullied him into couplehood, bundling him onto a ship bound for what she intended as a romantic retreat in Majorca and then nursing him through the dysentery he immediately contracted. George always got what she wanted, not always to her benefit (like... well, you can decide for yourself after you've read the book).

Offered a choice between manhood and womanhood, marriage and promiscuity, domesticity and passion, lust and maternal tenderness, George's answer was always and wholeheartedly: yes.

She died in 1876, after a final visit from her last great love Gustave Flaubert, who greeted her, as usual, "Oh you, of the third sex!" She was survived by her children and by many, many lovers.

I wish I'd gone to class that day.

nce a month or so I'd Greyhound across the mountains and spend the weekend with Candi — now calling herself Cat — in her dorm at Stanford. We'd lounge around her room smoking her excellent pot and listening to David Bowie and the New York Dolls on the stereo. "I'm soooo huuuuunnnngry," I'd moan. Cat would laugh and give me yet another set of directions to the student union where cookies could be purchased, and I'd stagger blinking out into the quad. Sometimes I'd wander for hours before finding my way back.

Cat's friends — the rangy girl-jock we'd gone to high school with, the round little androgyne she'd slept with once before he decided to stick with boys — often joined us for a toke or two. Everybody knew that I'd tried several times to lose my cherry and hadn't, and they teased me about it, usually when I was too stoned to notice that they were kidding.

After one of these weekends, I walked into the campus health clinic and had the offending bit of tissue breached by a scalpel-wielding doctor. The next night I grabbed Mike, the guy down the hall who painted his tennies with white shoe polish and hated everything about Santa Cruz and missed his girlfriend back in Visalia, and we tested out the new improved orifice. It still hurt and I bled a lot, but I had unquestionably had sexual intercourse.

here are three ways to have a penis between your legs. You can be born with one. You can fuck one. Or you can give birth to one. As of February 1973, my score was one out of three.

One night back at school, as I was leaving the cafeteria, trying to figure out where I could go that wasn't my empty, messy room, I saw a card on the bulletin board:

BRIDGE PLAYER WANTED
THREE PLAYERS LOOKING FOR A FOURTH FOR
WEEKLY GAME — CALL SCOTT, X8743.

Scott, it turned out, was a tall blond econ major with an ambitious vulpine grin, the kind of guy who would have been a superstar at UCLA but at Santa Cruz just seemed odd. Maureen was dark and slender, one of the few female math students in the college. Frank, studying chemistry, was short, broad-shouldered and heavy-browed, with angry eczematous skin, and spoke only to bid. The four of us wound up playing cards — gin or hearts when we tired of bridge — almost every night, often piling into Scott's Beetle for a trip downtown for doughnuts at 3 a.m. and more cards afterward.

I'd tried coming on to Scott, who'd gallantly pretended not to notice, so I was more or less "with" a guy named Barry who lived in the next dorm over from mine. The most appealing thing about Barry was that he thought I looked like Marthe Bonnard, the wife/muse of impressionist Pierre Bonnard — nobody had ever thought I looked like anybody before. Barry and I drew pictures of each other, and slept together, curled in the curve of each other's bodies, taking turns on the outside. We'd had sex twice, and since then Barry had always had a reason not to have it again.

Leaving his room after an argument on this subject one evening, I walked by the music practice room. Through the window I could see silent Frank playing the flute. The room was soundproofed and I could only hear the ghost of the tune, but with his lips pursed to make music, Frank had deep, humorous dimples in both cheeks.

I slept with Barry that night. I was still pissed off about the sex, but a warm bed is better than a cold one, and anyway I was pretty sure I was hatching a yeast infection. I was thinking, rather speculatively, about Frank, though.

*I*f my life were a musical, it wouldn't be one of the big, crowd-pleasing ones like *Oklahoma* or *South Pacific*, that tells you what you already know and gives you a little bit of safe controversy so you'll be able to tell your friends it had a message.

Instead, my life would be a cult favorite, off-off-Broadway at best. It would have a small cast, the kind where one person pops up over and over again in a different costume each time. Nobody would be relegated to the chorus and nobody would play a bit part; everybody would have their moment in the spotlight.

Two people might watch it together, on a date perhaps, and at the end one would think it was the stupidest thing they'd ever seen, and the other would walk home alone with her heart pounding and her brain buzzing, and there probably wouldn't be another date after that.

For that person, it would never again seem artificial for people to burst into song in the middle of a conversation. What would seem artificial is that they don't.

Yup, it was a yeast infection, the fourth in the year since I'd started taking birth control pills. There was one doctor in town who was willing to give the new effortless birth-control device, the Dalkon Shield, to girls who had never had a baby. His receptionist told me that I was to come in during my period, and that I needed someone to drive me home afterward.

Cat had a car. I called her. "Sure, I'll come," she said; I couldn't tell over the phone whether she was stoned or not. "But I need someone to fuck. If I'm going to come you have to get me someone to fuck."

This seemed sensible enough to me, but the logistics of the thing were a bit daunting: Mike and I hadn't spoken since he'd compared me negatively to the virginal girlfriend back in Visalia, and now I didn't even have anybody *I* could fuck. I pondered the issue and then asked Barry if he would please fuck Cat so I could get my IUD. He agreed, grinning, clearly feeling very bohemian.

She showed up on Wednesday night. The three of us ate a slightly awkward dinner together in the cafeteria. They left, holding hands, headed for his room.

I have no idea how I phrased my proposition to Frank — could I really have said "Hey, I just pimped out my boyfriend to my best friend for a ride to the doctor tomorrow, and I'm too lonely to sleep alone; wanna fuck?" — but at any rate, he said sure, why not.

He was a virgin, and my encounter with the scalpel was just a few months previous. The menstrual blood washed away whatever lubrication I might have been producing. The twin-sized steel bed somehow seemed to hold more than four elbows, more than four knees; we swore, dozed, tried again, failed. The sheets were a bloody wreck and Frank was trembling with nerves and frustration.

The next day Cat said goodbye to Barry and went back to Stanford, but that night I slept with Frank again. I was miserable with cramps from my newly installed IUD but we huddled together like kids at camp and talked long into the night. His frustration must have been nearly intolerable but he waited two more nights until the cramps subsided. Then we did it. The next week school was over and we both went home for the summer.

*T*he thing about that first summer home from college is that you've spent nine whole months being reborn as this new person, and then you go home and nothing has changed, especially you.

It was a quiet, warm, oddly slow-motion summer after the rackety discord of Santa Cruz. I sat up every night reading science fiction paperbacks or watching old movies, and slept until midafternoon. The house was usually empty when I woke up, so still that I could see pale dust motes floating in the balmy Southern California air.

My mother, nearing forty, had gone back to school with the intention of working on an accounting degree — but then she had taken Psych 1 and everything had changed. That was the summer she knew she wanted to be a therapist, so she was spending most of her time volunteering in a battered old trailer on campus that everybody called the "Help Center." I would come home after an afternoon at the beach with Cat or a night babysitting for the little blond toddler up the street, and see through the front window that the living room was full of earnest Help Center acolytes having an all-night encounter group — gesticulating, hugging each other, crying. I'd tiptoe around the front of the house and into the garage to let myself into the kitchen, trying to tune out the sound of confessions and shouts and sobs from the next room as I spread peanut butter and jelly on bread, then went outdoors again to take the sandwich back to my bedroom and close the door behind me.

The last time I'd seen Mom that happy, she'd been wearing yellow-tinted sunglasses and a sun visor and a khaki vest with lots of pockets, with a shotgun jauntily tipped across her shoulder: that's what she was wearing when she won the national women's trapshooting title early in the 1960s and appeared on the cover of *Trap & Field Magazine*. She wore the same proud smile in the photos she brought home from the Israeli Maccabiah Games, the Jewish Olympics — although in those she was dressed in a man's seersucker summer suit altered to fit her plump figure (it had never occurred to the team's uniform designer that a woman might shoot trap). She'd spent the week before leaving for Haifa frantically practicing the four-in-hand knot in her narrow navy-blue necktie.

Mom's road to Israel had started in suburban Philadelphia not long after my birth, when one of my dad's buddies invited him out trapshooting. The gun had kicked his face and shoulder into hamburger, he'd missed every shot, and he couldn't wait to go do it all again. Mom, who knew an obsession when she saw one, figured if she ever wanted to see her husband again she'd better take up the sport too.

That's how I wound up spending almost every summer weekend of my childhood bored to catatonia and mainlining Yoo Hoo Chocolate Beverages at gun clubs throughout eastern Pennsylvania, Delaware and New Jersey. But while I was running out of comic books by 11 a.m., Mom and Dad were climbing the national championship trapshooting rankings — Mom a little faster than Dad. The mid-'60s was not a time in which wives were supposed to be better at things than their husbands, but every weekend Mom shrugged off her suburban skirts and pumps, changed into slacks and a shooter's vest, and came home with trophy after trophy.

While she was in Israel, Mom learned to make a wonderful chopped salad with tomatoes and cucumbers and hard-boiled eggs, discovered "this amazing bread with a pocket in the middle — you know, if I could bake it here we could make a fortune with it," and fell volcanically and platonically in love with a handsome young revolutionary who was on the Israeli rifle team and who didn't care if she shot better than he did.

Kids rarely notice when their parents' lives have been turned upside down, but I really liked that salad.

My folks hung up their guns soon after the second Israel trip; when anybody asked, they said trapshooting had gotten too expensive. Mom messed around with macramé sculpture and then with home-baked bread, but she didn't find anything else she was really good at until nearly a decade later, when our move to Southern California and the complexities of the free-love-cheap-drugs era put her at the front desk of the Help Center.

One of the Help Center guys turned out to be the one person in the world with the patience to teach me how to drive a car. He was hoping to have sex with me, but I turned him down. Several of the others had similar ambitions — possibly hoping to connect with some aspect of my mother, without having to confront the physical reality of middle age or the oedipal reality of my dad — and took me to beach parties and movies. I liked getting taken to things, but it was just too creepy to contemplate having sex with a friend of my mother's. Nobody shared my bed that summer, but a

few of the beans from the beanbag Paul gave me were
still rolling around in the corners of my bedroom.

This morning, once again, the whine of the clippers separated me from me — in strands, then in small clumps, finally in a sifting itchy powder that clung to my neck and shoulders as if trying to climb back up and reattach itself.

I tipped the mirror this way and that, gauging my progress. I craned, searching for the proper angle, the one that shows what I want to see.

It wasn't there; it never is. Sighing, I swept myself up into a furry dustpan nest, and tipped myself into the garbage.

rank and I wrote each other all summer long, that first summer. He was on the first rung of the ladder of the family civil engineering business; he drove for hours in the valley heat to California's dustiest, most rural locations, then spent his day supervising the function of a gigantic machine that pounded a huge auger into the earth with a skull-ringing crash, over and over again, all day long. He wrote that he had actually sunburned his eyelids. The margins of his letters were full of little drawings and jokes in his tiny crabbed printing. Sometimes the letters themselves were dusty. They arrived almost every day, postmarked Colusa, Gualala, Yreka. I cherished them as evidence: it was the first time a guy had ever actually seemed to *want* to be in a relationship with me.

ow, in my fifties, like many formerly plain girls, I've learned to play the hand I was dealt: in a good light I might be called "handsome" or another of those middle-aged adjectives.

But I wonder sometimes what my life would have been like if I'd been pretty. Not handsome, not striking, not interesting-looking – pretty.

I try to imagine it: maybe a slight reshuffling of the chromosomes, maybe an early taste for green salad instead of Mystic Mints, maybe a benevolent fairy – subtracting an inch or two from my waist and adding it to the length of my legs, tightening my jawline and bumping out my cheekbones and fluffing up my hair and narrowing my forehead.

What then, I wonder?

Would I have been the kind of woman who waits to be asked, instead of the kind who does the asking? Or would I have still craved the power of being the initiator?

Would I have discarded men according to whim, trying out a dozen or a hundred or a thousand instead of grabbing the first amenable one? Or would I have projected that pretty-girl-don't-touch vibe, so that the first man courageous enough to approach me would be in fact the right one?

If I'd been pretty, would I ever have wondered, for one unguarded moment between sleep and waking: Whose woman-body is this? Where did these breasts came from, these soft thighs, this plump slitted pouch?

Or is it only plain girls who do that?

*S*ylvia, daughter of a Brooklyn dentist, was plain: plump, long-nosed, coarse-haired. David, the dentist's assistant, was redheaded and gangly, with a bright grin and nimble, long-fingered hands.

A decade later, they had become a team that would last until death parted them: Danny Kaye, comic superstar, and Sylvia Fine Kaye, his composer/lyricist, accompanist, manager and wife.

Sylvia wrote Danny's breakthrough hit, "Anatole of Paris" — in which he sang the part of an effeminate hat designer, back in the heyday of outrageous hats for women, when a hat could indeed cause "six divorces" and "three runaway horses." Danny sang "Anatole" as a young Catskills comedian, he sang it on his first record, he sang it in *The Secret Life of Walter Mitty*, he sang it to standing-room crowds at the Palladium. It's not too much to say that "Anatole" made Danny who he was.

Sylvia went on to write many more songs like this, songs that cast Danny as — not to put too fine a point on it — a screaming queen. Danny's curly red mop, graceful body and elegant hands made her task an easy one. Moss Hart finished the job when he cast Danny in the role that made him famous, as the epicene fashion photographer in *Lady in the Dark*.

Nobody knows who Danny would have been without Sylvia. He didn't need her romantically: they say his lovers included comedienne Eve Arden, dancer Gwen Verdon, and, most notoriously, Sir Laurence Olivier. Yet he was married to her till the day he died.

Hart's words in Danny's mouth in *Hans Christian Andersen:* "You'd be surprised how many kings are only a queen with a mustache." (I wonder if the original script said "beard.")

Here's what I think. I think Sylvia made Danny the star she could never be — graceful, androgynous, legendary. I think it was Sylvia who dressed Danny in stunning drag, as the cabaret singer Kay Thompson, to appear in front of Olivier at a charity benefit.

I imagine Sylvia's blunt short-nailed fingers smoothing the sleek jersey sheath down over Danny's taut buttocks. I imagine her tenderly massaging pomade into the red mop, slicking it back into a stylish auburn bob. I imagine her applying lipstick to the mobile mouth, then kissing Danny quickly on the cheek and sending him out into the lights.

I imagine Sylvia standing backstage, face impassive, watching Olivier laugh and cheer and applaud.

*T*he other thing about that first summer home from college is that the *you*-shaped hole in the family has been slowly closing for nine months, and you don't quite fit any more. Another year and it may be gone, although you don't know that at the time.

A lot of my music that summer was the kind of angsty folk-tinged stuff that young white girls with poetic aspirations listened to back then – Leonard Cohen, Joni Mitchell, Cat Stevens. But some combination of need and irony kept drawing me to the handful of Broadway cast albums in my parents' record cabinet. Most of these were the usual Golden Age standards – *My Fair Lady, Camelot, Carousel. Milk and Honey* as a nod to my mother's ancestry. *Jesus Christ Superstar* for a touch of hipness. *Annie Get Your Gun* because it was about shooting. I played them all.

But the one I reached for most often was a white-jacketed album featuring a cartoon of a man with his face painted like a mime, standing on a little globe. He was trying to walk forward, but a female hand was reaching in from outside the frame, grabbing his suspenders and pulling him backward: *Stop the World, I Want to Get Off.*

One weekend when I was seven or eight, my folks had hired a sitter and taken off for a romantic trip to New York — visiting my aunt and uncle, eating in restaurants better than the suburbs could offer, seeing the hottest new Broadway show, and, I'm sure, enjoying the short break from my sister and me. They came home with boxes of fancy candy for us, and a new album for everybody.

I loved this record, begging for it over and over, long after everyone else was sick of it. I was fascinated and envious: my parents had seen with their own eyes these actual people, singing these same songs, on a stage, in a real theater, in New York! I suppose some vestige of that glamour must have clung to the album a decade later, because I was still listening to it in the summer of '73.

I am now roughly twice as old as my parents were when they spent hard-won money on the romantic-weekend-alone-together solution for a failing marriage. I've been listening to that show for four and a half decades. The tunes are all grooved deeply into my brain cells: "Once In a Lifetime," "Lumbered," "What Kind of Fool Am I?" — big songs about a little, ordinary life, disquisitions on the era's newly-spoken unhappiness.

The last time I listened to this album, just last week, I noticed something for the first time. *Stop the World* is about a man who impregnates a woman from a different social class, is forced to marry her, has daughters with her but no sons, and trashes the marriage by obsessively having affairs. How could I have missed this?

When I listen to *Stop the World* from now on, I won't picture Anthony Newley and Anna Quayle. I'll see my parents, heartbreakingly young, my mother's round olive-skinned face and my father's narrow pale one, lit from above by the footlights. I imagine them holding hands.

Was it Mom or Dad, I wonder, who decided to buy that album and bring it home? And what passed through their minds as I insisted on playing it again and again?

The chorus in that musical is sung by the couple's daughters. I suppose that's me, now.

The show ends with the hero realizing that he's loved his wife all along and that his true source of happiness has always been his home, wife and children. That's the theater part, I guess.

*T*hat summer we had an invited visitor, my father's brother, an Episcopalian minister. And then we had two uninvited ones: Paul and his current boyfriend, a shy dreadlocked lad whose dark skin shone almost purple because the two of them had been sleeping on the streets like the Lost Boys in the southern California sun.

They crashed in my parents' back yard that night, snuggled together in an old half-zipped sleeping bag, their four feet — clad in matching purple socks — sprawled on the carefully tended dichondra. The next morning they asked if they could use our shower — showers, they said, were hard to come by for them right now. Of course, I said, and led them to the big shower adjoining my parents' bedroom. They began to peel off their grubby clothes and I turned to leave — but Paul asked, teasingly, "Aren't you going to join us?"

The water made everything so sweet and simple. Three heads, curly, straight, ropy, all drenched and dripping. Six hands, coffee, freckled, ivory, all busy and soapy. Three skins, all slippery-smooth in the steamy cascade. Two penises, four balls, two breasts, six nipples. Everybody washed everybody, brazen and innocent as babies in a wading pool, giggling and squealing and kissing.

We played and soaped and rinsed, the three of us, until the hot water ran out. My parents, who loved Paul too, frantically worked to distract my uncle from the splashing and shrieks coming from the bathroom.

If I'd known I'd never see Paul again, I'd have stayed in that shower forever. No matter who he brought with him, no matter who was visiting, no matter how cold the water got.

*T*he lights blaze down on the big, bare stage. The horns begin, slow, sad, seductive. The tiny figure at center stage grasps the microphone and begins to sing in a pure true voice, its edge rasped with sorrow and amphetamines.

The road gets rougher,
It's lonelier and tougher.
With hope you burn up —
Tomorrow he may turn up...

Is it Judy? Is it Rufus? Rufus wishing he were Judy? Judy wishing she were Rufus? The audience goes mad, shrieking, cheering, whistling, and it really doesn't matter, has never mattered, will never matter: the man got away.

ally Bowles, the protagonist of *Cabaret*, had big, dark, tragic eyes, and so did I. Sally Bowles had a veneer of sophistication that fooled nobody, and so did I. Sally Bowles *wanted* — men, money, fame, love, glamour — and so did I. If Sally Bowles could do it, I thought, so could I.

Sally, I knew, had plotted the seduction of her roommate Brian, choosing a slip of lace-trimmed champagne silk and a pair of Cuban-heeled pumps, feigning a chill to ask for a cuddle. Although my old high school buddy Russell resembled Brian — both were reserved, blond, slightly epicene university students — and although I'd known Russell much longer than Sally had known Brian, I had a feeling that he'd run screaming from the room if I showed up in anything that revealing. And besides, I reasoned, Russell hadn't had a couple of months in Berlin to warm him up; he was just coming over from Stanford for one night. I chose demure white cotton at the fabric store, sat up all night trimming it with flirty lace, and hemmed it long enough to provide plausible deniability if my nerve failed me.

We came back from the movies and I disappeared into the bathroom. When I appeared in the bedroom door, makeup freshened, bob brushed to shiny perfection, white lace fluttering around my thighs,

Russell looked up briefly, nodded a casual greeting and went on unrolling his sleeping bag.

"I... I thought we might share my bed," I said. (Sally, at this point, sprawled in an odalisque pose practically in Brian's face, and purred, "Doesn't my body drive you wild with desire?" It helps to have a screenwriter in these matters.)

"I think I'd be more comfortable here," Russell said, not meeting my eyes.

"But I thought maybe we could have sex," I whined.

"What is there about the word 'gay' that isn't clear to you?" Russell asked.

So I began to argue. That's how young I was: I thought you could argue someone into bed. I argued for hours. I even cried a little, which worked for Sally, eventually, but Russell slept in his sleeping bag.

I dropped out of Santa Cruz and moved to Davis. I proved that I could get married if I wanted to.

Some combination of need and irony made me ask Frank to marry me, and he said sure, why not. I picked the church, the bridesmaids, the groomsmen, the rings, the reception hall, the menu. Someone wanted me enough to marry me, and I wanted everyone to see, Cat and Barry and Russell and, well, everyone.

Frank was fine with whatever I wanted, coming along on appointments when I asked him to, staying home when I didn't. The morning of the wedding, though, he shaved his sensitive skin to a fiery glow, and looked callow and handsome and uncomfortable in his tux.

The ceremony was in his family's church, a little building so modestly Presbyterian that it was almost invisible. I hadn't wanted to buy my dress in a bridal shop because then it would look like a dress someone else was wearing somewhere else, so I'd found someone to sew one for me. In the end, though, it looked like anybody else's bridal gown: mandarin collar, princess seaming, ivory satin. My hair was too short to hold a headpiece, but I wanted a veil, so I attached one to a plastic headband that I'd covered with trim to match the dress.

My parents flew up from LA for the wedding. It was the last time I ever saw them together as a couple. They gave us a new queen-sized bed.

There was a murmur when Frank and I cut into our cake and everybody saw that it was chocolate. I'd figured that nobody really liked white cake anyway, and as long as it had white frosting on the outside and *looked* like a wedding cake, who cared what was on the inside?

All the people who had ridden in the station wagon to Paul's housewarming were at the wedding. Paul wasn't there, though, because I'd had no way to reach him. "I heard that he committed suicide," said Cat, and I didn't have time to feel sad, because after all it was just a rumor, and besides, I had to go dance with my new father-in-law.

II

A LITTLE HOUSE WHERE
I CAN TELL STORIES

How can I tell you about myself with the words I have? Danny Kaye was a "man." George Sand was a "woman" ("the most womanly woman," in fact). Paul was "gay"; he said so. Frank was "straight."

But Candi became Cat — an animal whose gender is not apparent at first glance — and would someday become Carl, a handsome balding bearded fellow to whom I am still closer in many ways than anyone else in the world. Is he "gay" or "straight" now? Is he a "man" or a "woman"?

If I try to tell this story without these words, in which I no longer believe, it will make no sense.

It doesn't make much sense anyway, you say.

I say, but it's my story.

Nineteen sixty-two: The other girls hold their books with their arm bent somehow, so the books end up in front of them. I hold my books hanging down by my side. I try moving my arm this way and that, but can't figure out how they're doing it. One day when nobody is around, I carry some books into my parents' room and practice in front of the full-length mirror until I figure out the trick of bending my arm upward so that it crosses my chest and my books are pressed coyly against what will someday be my breasts.

1968: Jeannie at Girl Scouts, who has been to charm school, stands with her shoulders back, chin level, left leg straight but not locked, and her right heel to her left instep, knee bent, foot turned out at a thirty-degree angle. It makes her look extremely elegant and adult. Back to the mirror.

1971: Candi and I are going to the mall in hopes of meeting some cute guys. "Show me your walk," she demands. I walk for her, attempting the slouching shimmy of that miniskirted era. *"That's* not very sexy," she tells me. "Do it again." I accept her authority meekly; she clearly knows much more than I do about how to be sexy. I practice until she shrugs ungraciously and says it's going to have to do.

1999: I attend a baby shower at which the mother-to-be is dressed comfortably in bib-front denim overalls and sturdy work boots. His ZZ Top beard is brushing the top of his nine-months' belly. He thanks us, in a gravelly baritone, for coming. He explains that he has decided to take a hiatus during his female-to-male gender transition — the next step is a hysterectomy, and he wants a baby before that happens. I applaud politely as he opens his gifts, and feel confused, and happy.

Remember, please, the first woman you ever wanted.

The curve of shoulder, the drift of hair, the weight of breast, the soft ineffable voice. Welcoming skin, softness intolerable, open invitation.

How does she cross her legs, what weight presses thigh to thigh? What sound does she make, what little stutter or *tsk* or intake of breath, to tell you she is about to start speaking? What lusts shape her lips before she opens them to accept a morsel? What unplumbed folds, what journeys, lie between her legs?

Now: become her. Move inside her skin. Feel your breasts sway, soft and certain as gravity. Touch your arm, feel its heat under your marveling hand. Run your tongue along your upper lip, so downy-strange, so perfectly familiar, this lip that you have known for as long as you've known anything.

You are the seer, dreaming of who knows what impossible congresses. You are the seen, lust omnipresent as silk on skin, tiny hairs erecting along your nape and forearms.

One does not exist without the other.

Remember, please, the first woman you ever wanted to be.

She is the sun, filling past and future, erasing the memory of cold. She knows what nobody can know, and contains it with what may or may not be a smile. Her beauty, effortless, inherent, reflects and negates every picture of beauty you've seen. She could give birth to any fantasy that's ever soothed waking to sleep, or she could annihilate with a word.

Can you see how she curves her hand, gently encircling with her fingers an apple, a pen, a baby bird, a heart? Can you remember how closely you watched her, trying to discern the secret of how to be her?

Now: enter her. Feel her volcanic complicated core fluttering and clenching around you. Its darkness and heat transport you. You are welcome here, you are pulled in deeper. You are bounded and embraced and compressed. This is a path you have traveled, are traveling, will always travel; this is the path that defines you.

You are the lover, the perfect fit, the missing part, the key. You are the beloved, completed, engulfing, infinite.

One does not exist without the other.

Remember, please, the first man you ever wanted to be.

A hero he is, brave and beautiful, capable and kind. A man who can lift a child like you up to the sky, and when he sets you down again you'll be older, taller, better. His eyes take you in, hold you, warm you. His hands can build or direct or soothe, hands that feel everything they touch, hands that frighten you a little in a way you don't understand.

Can you see how the cords of his back rise and fall under his shirt, sure and unpredictable as wind? Can you remember how closely you watched him, trying to discern the secret of how to be him?

Now: devour him. Feel him swell in your mouth; he seems nearly too much, but you can hold him: it was he who gave you the size you need to contain him. His groans shake your skeleton, massage your heart. Your throat is full and you no longer have any holes. You are complete; by taking him in, you have recreated yourself.

You are the lover, the receptacle, single-purposed, insatiable. You are the beloved, immense, incomprehensible.

One does not exist without the other.

Remember, please, the first man you ever wanted.

Pattern of sinew and vein at turn of wrist. Soft hairs spiraling into mysterious navel. Scapulae that spread like archangel wings when he reaches out for the thing he wants. Voice, that voice, granular and certain except in the wavering moments that haunt you.

What is the smell of his mysterious nape, where the capital W of hair separates head from muscular neck? If you seize that ridge at the front of the armpit, thumb in the damp hairs, fingers cupping the swelling of shoulder, will he flinch or succumb?

Now: become him. Move inside his skin. Your adam's apple a jumpy warm complicated pebble, restive under your fingertips. Your feet, five springy bridges of agile bone; your stride, effortless and gravity-defying. Soft full creatures shift and adjust between your legs, silent and demanding.

You are the seer, dreaming of who knows what impossible congresses. You are the seen, wary and flattered, suspended between flight and surrender.

One does not exist without the other.

I wasn't very good at the wife thing, as it turned out. The one thing a wife did that I knew how to do too was cook.

Every week I made a list of the coming week's meals, then sat down with a piece of paper divided up into columns and made a complete shopping list of everything we'd need. We went through the Crepe Phase, in which everything I made came rolled up in an eggy golden epidermis; the Homemade Bread phase, in which we both gained weight because the moment the two fragrant loaves came out of the oven we'd consume them both, heavily buttered, in minutes; the Ethnic Phase, in which I bought cookbooks that taught Americanized versions of classic Greek, Thai, Japanese and Chinese dishes; and innumerable short-lived Healthy Phases, in which I tried to figure out ways to make vegetables and chicken breasts delicious enough to substitute for our usual rich delights.

Meanwhile, weeks' worth of newspapers and soda cans piled up in corners, and drifts of cat and dog hair settled over all our thrift-store furniture.

here's a game I like to play when I'm in airports and places like that, places with a lot of different kinds of people intent on their own business. You can't play it in a place where people are looking back at you, because it requires that you gaze at them intently and that makes them nervous: you'll get to see a lot of fly-checking and hair-patting, but you won't get much of a game out of it. It's better if you can sit off to one side, out of people's line of sight, and see without being seen.

It's pretty simple. For each person who walks by, you imagine: If this person were my lover, what is the thing about them that would make my knees go weak? That guy has fluffy gray hair that I think I'd want to run my fingers through a lot. That woman has a long stride that looks like she owns the ground she walks on. I would do anything to see that dimpled smile over and over again. *Look* at those hands, how mobile and delicate and curved, like a Michelangelo drawing, what would it feel like to have those hands on my skin?

Most people want to play my game with exclusions: no men, no women, no fat people, no old people, no teenagers, whatever. If you think you can play the game that way, then you don't understand the game and you're not allowed to play it.

*H*is bare feet are spread wide, rooted to the floor with the certainty of archetype. Draped silk trousers frame his muscular calves and his strong arms are crossed in front of his gleaming bare chest. His head is naked, long-templed, round-crowned. His back is slightly arched, as though he must balance the weight of his genitals.

Who am I describing? Why, me, obviously.

No, it's Yul Brynner.

No. Yul Brynner was born Yuli Borisovich Bryner, in Vladivostok in 1915, and acted in Westerns and Biblical epics and art films, and died of lung cancer at seventy.

It's King Mongkut of Siam.

No. King Mongkut founded an order of Buddhism, offered elephants to James Buchanan, and made his courtiers wear shirts.

It is, of course, the sublime King of Siam in *The King and I:* an endlessly fascinating and contradictory package of virility and uncertainty, tenderness and arrogance, all wrapped up in silk and machismo.

The King's vest is trimmed ornately in gold – he is, after all, the King – but he seems always on the verge of tearing it off, of leaping naked into some savage dance that only a man can dance. There is a moment in the film, the moment when he first touches Anna's waist, a simple touch over so many layers of taffeta and corsetry that she probably can't even feel it, and it's like a lightning bolt has leapt from the screen to paralyze me where I sit, that simple hungry touch that bridges race and culture, power and resistance, virility and femininity.

This man, this King, does not exist, not in any world I've ever been allowed to live in. It doesn't matter.

This is the man I want to be. The man I want to fuck. The man I want to own. The man.

I'm told that in drag I look like Sigmund Freud. Freud said, "Anatomy is destiny." I bet Freud would rather have been Yul Brynner, too. Or Kay Thompson, for that matter.

*G*ay men, I've found, are the best for flirting with. They know the rhythm: the self-revelation, the personal observation, the compliment, the touch, reeling you in, giving you slack, pulling you back in again. Flirting with gay men is lighthearted, consequence-free, an easy ritual.

When you try to flirt with straight guys, there's always the chance that the flirtation might turn into actual sex. Flirtation becomes a kind of playing chicken — how far can you take it before someone makes an actual proposal, before someone has to say yes or no?

The fact is that even when you flirt with a gay man, sex isn't necessarily all that distant a possibility; such things have been known to happen. But his gayness gives the flirtation some plausible deniability. You can flirt with impunity, which means you can flirt very well indeed.

If you're worried that you're too old or too fat or too unattractive, then you're not going to be flirting very well — in fact, you probably won't be flirting at all. Confident people flirt; insecure people beg. When you flirt with a gay man, he's not supposed to notice what you look like because of course he isn't going to fuck you anyway, so you can just go for it.

You know who else is really great at flirting? Babies. If you want proof that great flirting is an end in itself, consider this scenario: you're sitting there in the diner having a cup of coffee and reading the paper, and suddenly over the top of the banquette in front of you appears a pair of enormous blue eyes. You smile, or make a face, or stick out your tongue, and the eyes disappear bashfully behind the red vinyl, and you hear a muffled giggle. You go back to your newspaper but now you can't really concentrate: she's got you. And sure enough, a tuft of fluffy hair rises up, followed by a round forehead, and again those big eyes, now crinkled with merriment.

From here on out you're hooked; you can forget about the newspaper. You'll be making faces, playing peekaboo, performing puppet shows with your slices of bacon: babies are not always so good at figuring out when to *stop* flirting. But they are superb at starting, and even better at continuing, which are, after all, the hard parts.

But, you know, a baby isn't tall enough to see over the back of a banquette. All that fabulous flirtation is performed standing on the lap of a loving parent who will pick her up and soothe her if someone, say, sticks a couple of straws up their nose to be a walrus and startles her and makes her cry. Flirt with The Weird Lady In The Restaurant; get comforted by Mommy. It's the perfect, safe setup. Like being gay, but with looser pants.

*C*at was married too, and I missed her a lot. Frank and I saved up Coke bottles and spare change to buy plane tickets, and flew East to visit her and her new husband in their dilapidated little house near Brown University.

From behind, Cat and Andy looked like twins: waist-length hair, broad shoulders, thick waists, powerful legs. Andy was a grad student in math, Cat was stocking shelves in a grocery co-op. Every corner of their house was piled with books, cigarettes, dishes and beer cans, but they'd made space in a corner of the living room for a single mattress on the floor for Frank and me. We sat side-by-side on it, beers in hand, and they sat in the two sagging easy chairs that were the dark little room's only real furniture. We were on our second joint already.

"I can't believe you guys didn't even tell us you were getting married," I chided.

"Well, it was kind of a spur-of-the-moment thing," Cat said. "Here, look." She handed me a ragged stack of snapshots. In one, Andy was being handed the ring by a slender curly-haired young woman dressed in a Goodwill tux; she seemed to be acting as best man. "I met her at the co-op," Cat explained. "We've been lovers for a year or two now." Andy smiled benignly, took another hit off his joint, and passed it along to Frank. "Cool!" I exclaimed, brightly and uncertainly.

By the third joint, everyone had reached the point where staring at the ceiling was more interesting than talking, only I seemed to have rolled over onto my side, so I was staring at a messy pile of books instead. Most were thick, hardcover math texts, but a few paperbacks were in there too. One caught my eye: *The Adventures of Janet*. I pulled it from the pile, dislodging a crusty empty coffee mug which rolled away unnoticed. The book's cover was plain lime green with cheap typography. "What's this?" I asked.

Cat and Andy started to giggle. "Oh, that," Cat said. "It's this hilarious porn book, someone left it in the co-op and I swiped it out of the lost and found box..." We all drifted away again.

Glancing through the book, I discovered that its structure was straightforward: it had one chapter for every kind of sex I could imagine. "He spat on his forefinger and lubricated her furtive rosebud..." I flipped forward a few pages.

"Scarcely able to believe her good fortune, she caressedMelanie's heavy, pink-tipped breasts..."

"Held immobile by the sturdy rope around her wrists and ankles, she gazed up helplessly at his rampant manhood..."

I started to close the book, but as the pages flipped by, a word leaped up: *spank*. I looked around to see if anyone had heard me make a sound, but apparently nobody had, or maybe the sound didn't exist outside the world of pot-fueled paranoia. I leafed through the book trying to find that page again. Yes, there it was: the hero had just decided that the pink handprints on the heroine's buttocks weren't enough, and had picked up a hairbrush. I blushed deeply, and not only in my face. Quietly, I dog-eared the page and put the book back on its pile.

Late that night, when everyone was asleep, I tiptoed back out into the living room and read the chapter through twice. I found it easy enough to transpose the heroine's gender to male as I read, particularly since I wasn't very interested in the fucking part at the end. Once I'd made that adjustment, the chapter read very much like the stories that had distracted my waking hours since earliest memory. I was more than just turned on – I was illuminated: my stories, my private dramas, were about *sex*.

I read the chapter through a third time, but by then the excitement was wearing off, so I unfolded my dogear and put the book away.

As I slipped back under the covers next to Frank, I thought about waking him up to share my new discovery, but I was pretty sure he wouldn't understand; or, worse, that he might laugh at me; or, worse yet, that he might just want to fuck. I closed my eyes and tried to go to sleep, but I wound up lying there awake for a long time.

*T*hey say all great narratives start with some variation on "Unbeknownst to him/her…"

So: Unbeknownst to me, within a few miles of where I leafed through that paperback, a future friend and colleague was helping to create a whole new genre of erotica, and acknowledging a sexual orientation undreamed of by doctors Freud, Kinsey et al.

I wasn't to discover slash fiction for two more decades. When I finally did, I stared in amazement as the screen of my computer filled over and over again with fantasies just like the ones that had filled my adolescence: men and men, penitence and redemption, innocence given and taken, pain and nurturing. Where was this when I needed it? Why did I feel so alone for so long?

Slash fiction got its start, of course, on *Star Trek* — the "slash" stands for the virgule in "K/S," or "Kirk/Spock." (I do remember having such fantasies at the time, although Kirk never interested me much.) The original slash was homegrown, woman-created erotica based on the Paramount characters, in which Kirk's bombastic virility and Spock's lean asceticism are brought together into passionate fucking, sucking, fisting, rimming, flogging and every other form of eroticism known to men and imagined by women.

Isaac Asimov famously opined that sexy Spock bore primary responsibility for bringing women into the science fiction community, and at least in my case I think he had a point.

According to my friend Cecilia Tan, one of the pioneers of the genre, such tales were being written and shared in the science fiction community as far back as the early 1970s, in photocopied zines that were shared — without the consent of Paramount and the other corporate entities that held the copyrights to the characters — at conventions and other gatherings. "Although 'slash' didn't originally imply only gay pairings," she tells me, "since then male-male sex has become the default — if you write heterosexual stuff you have to label it as 'het', and female-on-female sex gets called 'femmeslash'."

Where was I while all this was going on? Oh, yes, being a wife and mom. I remember now.

Slash was an underground current in science fiction for many years, influencing the writing of many well-known genre writers such as Marion Zimmer Bradley and Joanna Russ without ever breaking through into the consciousness of the mainstream. Until, of course, the Internet.

The Internet turned slash into a worldwide phenomenon, finally bringing it enough into the mainstream that even middle-aged women like me could find it. It's almost impossible to imagine any pairing from literature or pop culture that hasn't taken over someone's erotic imagination — I was taken aback to discover a small but rich vein of Pan/Hook slash. And the more active communities, like Harry Potter and *Buffy the Vampire Slayer,* include thousands of tales, some of them full-length novels with six-figure word counts. The erotic drive involved in writing a hundred-thousand-word novel, solely for one's own pleasure and the pleasure of sharing with like-minded others, is difficult for me to imagine; most people commit that kind of energy to having sex, not to writing about it. But Cecilia tells me that for her, and for many others, "Slash *is* our sexuality."

She doesn't mean that she writes slash instead of having sex; I know she has sex, a lot of it. She seems to mean instead that the values and ideals and conventions of slash fiction have informed her sex life, rather than the converse.

Slash has seeped out into the culture. I don't know who first pointed out that "Brokeback Mountain," both the original short story and the subsequent film, is essentially Marlboro Man slash, but once you see the connection you can't un-see it. (Cecilia doubts that author Annie Proulx was consciously making slash – which only goes to show you that girlfags are self-generating, needing no more outside influence than any other sexual orientation.) And gradually, those who make popular culture are learning that pandering to slash-lovers puts female butts into moistening seats: consider the later seasons of *Buffy*, with their not-all-that-carefully veiled homoerotic implications, or the magnificent slashiness of *Torchwood* or *Supernatural*.

The pervasiveness of slash has made waves in the gay world, too. The folks behind the Lambda Book Award, the premier honor given to GLBT literature, have wavered back and forth in their definition of what constitutes, for example, a gay male novel. If a novel is about gay men, goes the argument, does that make it a gay male novel? What if it feels real to gay male readers, if the love and affection and sex in it are true to the realities and fantasies of men who love men, but it was written by a woman? What if she uses a male or gender-neutral pen name, as so many female authors have, and you don't find out till later? What if the author is someone like Vita Sackville-West, or George Sand, or me?

I don't envy the Lammies this decision. I've never been able to make it myself.

*N*otes from an interview with K:

"Red corduroy pantsuit." She wore it when she was a child because it was the closest thing she could find to boys' clothes, wore it every day in spite of bribes from her grandfather to please for god's sake just put on a dress one damn time, wore it until it fell apart.

"Sex with my first husband." Infrequent but nice. It wasn't really a sexual relationship and it was difficult to make it be one, she says, because he wanted men and she wanted women.

"Missionary position." She will never be in it. This is, she says, not unproblematic. I take this statement to have a meaning broader than a simple arrangement of arms and legs.

"Dyke. Woman-identified but not femme. Other than female." These shadings of meaning make sense to me when I write them down, but when I try to parse them for you here, they don't.

"My first girlfriend." Kinky. Psychotic.

"The clearest manifestation of female energy in a male body I've ever encountered." She is describing my spouse Edward, her ex, still her good friend. She says the relationship was spectacular and that the relationship was complicated by the fact that she could not allow sex.

"Love of my life." Submissive crossdresser, very feminine. No genital relationship. Gone now.

"My current husband." Somewhere between crossdresser and transgendered. She complains: he moves clumsily, talks loudly, not observant, no sensitivity. Not womanly. The longest relationship she has ever had, fourteen years now.

"My future." Would have to be with a woman. There was a girlfriend last year; she would have left her husband for this woman. It didn't work out.

"My art." Visual, she says, but deeper, deeper than energetic, shaping essence. She sets up a ritual environment, candles, bondage, kneeling, both she and her work of art feeling as much as they can, quivering and sensitive, different, changing, being changed. She is writing her dissertation about art like this.

"I know what I want and I want it." What she wants, she says, is to create a woman where there was no woman.

"What I'd do with a woman…" She stumbles. Take a rest from shaping, she supposes.

*I*f you were here right now, here's how I'd flirt with you. I'd start with some sort of neutral observation: "Interesting book, huh?"

You'd respond with some sort of non-committal observation about the book. I'd escalate to the next step, the ever-so-slightly-too-intimate self-revelation: "Boy, when I read a book like that, it just makes me want to spend my life in gay bars, flirting."

You'd agree with me, or disagree, or contribute a little self-revelation of your own. I'd proceed to Step 3, the ever-so-slightly-too-personal compliment: "Well, when someone with boots *that* sexy enjoys the same book I enjoy, then I know I must be on the right track."

By now, surely one of us would have said something witty enough that you'd have laughed, or at least chuckled. (If not, it's time for me to pack up my gear and move on.) When I laughed along with you, I'd put my hand lightly on your forearm and make eye contact, just for a second, not in any intense meaningful this-is-going-somewhere way but more in an I-see-you-as-flirtworthy way.

And if you're a gay man, that's usually that. We've had fun, we've felt witty and urbane, we've each made the other believe that we're incredibly attractive, and it's time to get back to whatever, or whoever, it was we were doing. A win-win.

If you're a straight man, though, you're now either thinking "Oh boy I'm gonna get laid tonight" or "Oh shit how do I get rid of her?" There is a kind of flirting that's about that, but it's not the kind I'm talking about. That kind of flirting, the kind that you do with the intention of leading up to sex, is different. It ought to have a different name: Extreme Flirting, maybe. I can't really tell you much about that kind because I'm not very good at it — I'd probably get laid a lot more if I were. I'm more the so-you-wanna-fuck? kind of girl, which I'm here to tell you does not actually work all that well with straight men, who are, it seems, easily frightened.

Or maybe you're a gay man who occasionally sleeps with women. In which case, you know how to flirt, and you're available for sex. And here's what I have to say about that: my email address is janet@janetwhardy.com, and, yes, I own a strap-on.

*U*ncle Tim is not my actual uncle, nor is he my godfather. There should be a word for the individual who precipitates one's existence, who nudges the sperm toward the egg. One's third parent, perhaps. Or one's inspiration.

Dear Tim, my mother wrote in 1954. *I hope Haverford is more fun than Smith, because it's pretty bad here. All these thin blond girls seem to know each other, and know what they're doing here. There's a drama class I like pretty well but I think I might be failing German. Of course, it would help a lot if I didn't get soaked to the skin every time I step outside. Come visit me, you rat, and bring me my umbrella that you "borrowed" back in August. I miss you. Damply, Sue.*

My father — twenty years old, gangly, hairline already starting to recede a bit — is sprawled in Tim's desk chair, idly picking over the papers scattered on top of the desk. Tim is stretched out on the bed, glasses at the end of his nose, reading the same paragraph of Wittgenstein for the third time; it still doesn't make sense.

"Who's this Sue?" my father asks. "Is she cute?"

Tim gives up on the Wittgenstein and tosses it aside. "I guess, if you like that type. Pretty eyes. She was Katisha and I was the Mikado in our high school play. Why don't you go ahead and answer that letter? — I don't have time."

The path from that moment to my existence was shorter than you might imagine. A date in New York. A plump dreamy girl smitten with the kind of things that impress nineteen-year-old college sophomores (a packet of English Oval cigarettes, a bottle of wine ordered by vintage). A blanket spread on the grass because virgins didn't get into the back seat with boys. A panicky phone call four weeks later.

I have a reminiscence-filled email from Tim, sent as we planned my visit to the small Southern college town where he lives. *When Susan and Dick rushed into the marriage they received a number of wedding gifts that they didn't really want. I was given a few of them, as I was then setting up housekeeping. One of them has remained with me, and thus celebrates its "golden anniversary" this year. It's the Waring Blendor, two speeds, which Susan gave me after she'd dropped the glass container and broken it. I replaced the container and I've been using it ever since — it continues to churn up my cream soups.* The appliance he is describing is, of course, exactly my age.

Many of my earliest memories include Uncle Tim, sleeping on the couch in the den, splashing with my sister and me in our wading pool, arguing music with my father. He had a brush cut (unlike all the dads I knew, who had hair pomaded straight back from their foreheads), glasses with horn-rims (which fascinated me by being sort of transparent and sort of opaque, and besides, they had a *color,* unlike the somber dark rims worn by dads and the coquettish cat's-eyes worn by moms), and drove an odd, hunched-up little gray car that had its engine in the back. He treated me with exaggerated courtesy, kissing my small hand as though it belonged to Princess Grace.

By the time I started kindergarten, though, we didn't see Uncle Tim as often — he was in graduate school, I heard, and then traveling. But he showed up when I was in fourth grade, in transit from somewhere to somewhere else, with a companion, a lean silent young man who was going into the Army.

Mom faltered when I asked her about it in the privacy of my bedroom that night. "Um... the thing is... do you know what AC/DC means?"

I vaguely associated the sounds with the song *Mairzy Doats,* which I liked, but that didn't seem to make sense so I shook my head no.

"Hmmm, OK. Well... did you know that some men like to be in love with other men? They're called 'homosexuals'."

"No..."

"Well, and then there are other men and ladies who like both things, to be in love with men and to be in love with ladies. That's what AC/DC means. And so Tim's friend is... kind of like his wife."

(Tim writes: *I have no recollection of that visit. It may relate to my trip to California when I was changing jobs. I had a traveling companion, a casual friend, certainly not a lover, who had recently graduated from college and who came along to share the driving.* My mother says on the phone, "That's odd; I always thought Tim was gay, or at least bi." I notice that nowhere has he actually said otherwise, but I keep my mouth shut.)

Left alone in the darkness of my room, I pondered this new information with wonder and an odd sense of revelation. There was life, it seemed, beyond station wagons and well-kept lawns, bridge games and Dairy Queen.

Somewhere there were places where men had other men as their wives.

Where? I wondered. Probably in cities. Probably in New York. I'd visited my aunt and uncle in New York, gone up and down in fascinating elevators with gates on the front and big levers pulled by men in uniforms, looked awestruck through store windows at animated Christmas displays, been given exotic foods like watercress sandwiches and petits-fours and Brazil nuts. People in New York, I knew, were writers and painters and actors, and they went to the theater and saw plays, and stayed up as late as they wanted. People in New York asked you what your favorite books were, and smiled oddly when you said *The Black Stallion* and *Lad: A Dog,* and sent you Christmas packages containing books of poetry that didn't rhyme.

My best friend Kathy and I had already spent many hours deciding where we'd live when we grew up. We'd share a big house way out in the country, we knew, with many fenced yards, where we'd have dogs and cats and horses and turtles and birds and maybe even snakes. I'd be the artist and she'd be the writer, and we'd write and illustrate books together in time taken out from our work as veterinarians.

As I lay there in bed, though, the big house in the country slowly dissolved, and in its place I saw a tall skyscraper. A uniformed doorman bowed and opened the door, and there was a brass mailbox in the lobby that you unlocked with a special key and that was full of bright magazines and long handwritten letters from all over the world. A clanking iron elevator disgorged a stream of people into a high-windowed apartment, where they admired the big bright paintings on the walls, and drank cocktails with onions in them, and ate watercress sandwiches. Some of the men were married to each other, and nobody cared.

Soon afterward, I started looking at the unrhyming poems and trying to figure out why they were poems.

Tim writes, *Sonja, my wife, and I have now been married for 28 years. Not always easy, but, as I like to say, "we like the same things," so the relationship has been good.*

I go to visit him; I'm traveling through his area on business. He and Sonja have converted an industrial building into gorgeous, open space, with pale hardwood floors, walls aglow with rich russet and bottomless midnight blue, each chair and end table unique and hand-selected from a lifetime's travel. Two identical apricot toy poodles, one male, one female, both named George, stand on their hind legs and brace their tiny claws against my shins, trying to catch a glimpse of the Brie and sliced apples on the plate balanced on my knee.

Would I have recognized him on the street? Perhaps. The brush cut has been replaced by a wavy white mane worn combed back from the familiar high forehead. The glasses are steel-rimmed instead of horn-rimmed, and the round cheeks of youth have fallen in, leaving lines that reflect more frowning than smiling. But the slender build is the same, and so is the ponderous inflection in the speech, with a slight ironic dryness behind it that feels as familiar as my old twill twin-sized bedspread.

Tim takes me on a tour; we make a special stop in the well-appointed kitchen to visit my inorganic twin, the Waring Blendor. Part of the building has been divided and soundproofed as a music studio for Sonja, and another part is being rented to an artist. Most of it, though, is open space, lined with shelves and niches, each with its own little spotlight. These have been built for Tim's amazing collection of musical instruments from all over the world; although I know nothing about music, I can see that many are very old and, I suspect, valuable. The spotlights highlight the polished wood of a violin, the tarnished brass of an original sousaphone, the gleaming pale drumhead worn smooth by the beating of human hands. The pride of the collector shines in Tim's eyes as he tells me about them, how he acquired them, what they mean.

Sonja comes home; Tim quietly returns a drum to its niche. Sonja is small, concavely thin, with maroon hair cut short and styled with precision. She wears heavy handmade jewelry, her trademark, so massive that it seems her tiny frame must break under its weight. She is frazzled — a charitable project she's working on is going badly, nobody understands why it's important to do it the right way, she's been arguing all day with designers and money people.

She and Tim chat. I try not to look like I'm listening carefully, but I am, hoping to divine the nature of this relationship, listening for affection or exasperation or apathy. What I hear is the casual how-was-your-day debriefing of any long-married couple, unselfconscious, neither cool nor warm, the hum of a well-maintained engine.

Sonja disappears into the bedroom, trailed by George and George. She must change clothes; it seems we're having dinner with a family friend at her country club. "I'd be fine with just hanging out here and talking if you'd rather," I say hopefully. I have so many questions for this man: Who was my mother to you? My father? Do you often think of me, this life you started? Am I what you would have wished me to be? Is there another Tim somewhere, sipping espresso in Rome perhaps, laughing with a slender olive-skinned boy-man whose smile gleams in the hot sunshine? Who have you loved? What has made you happy?

I'm hungry for truth, but I'm going to get food instead — apparently the country club date cannot be cancelled. So I never get the chance to ask what I want to ask, or say what I want to say, or even to figure out exactly what I'd say if I could.

Sonja is ready to leave. When we open the front door, it is wet outside, with the sort of warm summer rain that Californians like me tend to forget is possible. Sonja has her own umbrella, so Tim gallantly offers me his arm, and we walk together to the car under his.

*I*as back in school, taking whatever classes I had to take to finish my degree, doing exactly the amount of work needed to earn a decent grade — no more, no less. Frank had already finished his degree and was working long hours as a junior engineer in the business his father built.

To our surprise, we discovered something else a wife did that I could do too. My breasts got so sore that I had to carry my schoolbooks down by my side again, and I didn't feel like eating any of the good food I'd cooked, and then I missed a period. My gynecologist bet me a 7-Up that I wasn't pregnant, but he never bought it for me. He did, however, take out my defeated IUD.

We discussed abortion, but I said what the hell, let's have it, and Frank said sure, why not. I didn't know how to be a mother but I was pretty sure I could figure it out as I went along.

We sold Frank's old Mustang and got a station wagon. Frank learned to sauté liver because I knew I was supposed to eat it but the smell of it made me gag. We bought a ramshackle little bungalow across the street from a junkyard in Sacramento because it had a clawfoot bathtub and a big shady tree in the back yard. Miles was born on Christmas Eve, a few weeks before my twenty-third birthday, and I was back in school in January to finish out my last two quarters, with Frank's mom watching the baby while I was in classes.

You can be born with one. You can fuck one. Or you can give birth to one. By 1978 I was two for three.

*H*ere's how to fly in slow motion:

First the baby latches on, which feels like a minor torture of the Inquisition, and you yelp and grit your teeth. And then, magically, this sneaky warm flood of sweetness starts at your breast and rushes outward to your fingers and feet and eyelids and groin, and everything slows down. It bathes you like sunlight, this rush; it makes you smile stupidly, makes you think the peppery smell of the baby's head is better than Chanel No. 5 and fresh-baked bread combined, makes you nod like a junkie in a rocking-chair stupor. And the baby feels it too, turns from a tense fussy bundle of elbows and knees into a soft, heavy, liquid weight, pressed to your skin as though he were ready to ooze back in through your pores and reoccupy you forever, eyes closed, hands dropping open, boneless and aimless except for the purposeful monotonous pulsing of tongue and gums and lips.

While you're doing this, you don't wonder whose breasts these are; you know. They're yours, and the baby's.

Sweetness this sharp makes everything else irrelevant. At least for a while.

*F*rank and I sold the house and bought a bigger one, then did it again, then did it again. I found jobs because typesetting had turned me into a blisteringly fast typist, talked bosses into letting me write ads and press releases, then got fired when I wouldn't let them rewrite my copy. Frank moved from junior engineer to staff engineer to vice president. Miles grew from infancy to toddlerhood to preschoolerhood, and we had Ben, on purpose this time.

A conversation, held exactly once:

Frank: "Was that kind of what you wanted? Was it OK?"

Me, breathlessly: "Yeah, pretty much. It was *awesome*. Next time maybe can we try it harder? With a hairbrush or something?"

Frank: "Um… well, maybe. I guess. If we fuck afterwards."

(A long pause.)

Frank: "But… can you try to kind of explain to me what it was you liked about it?"

There was never enough money. I bought clothes and shoes, appliances and expensive cuts of meat, gym memberships, new cars, toys for the kids, but nothing worked; I didn't even know what "working" would look like. We kept earning more and more, and checks kept bouncing and credit cards kept being declined.

One night I had a feeling, sort of like restless legs but all over my body, crawly and implacable. It felt sort of like I wanted to hit someone, and sort of like I wanted to get in the car and drive and drive and drive, and sort of like I wanted to explode. It came and it stayed, some nights worse, some nights better, but always there.

Orgasm didn't kill it: I masturbated until my hand cramped, and it was still there. Exercise didn't kill it: I worked out until I was trembling and nauseated, and it was still there. We'd put the boys to bed, and Frank would sit and smoke and read, and I'd pace around the house, sit down, do a little knitting or sewing, get up, pace some more, go for a walk, come back, pace some more, bake some cookies, eat them, and finally, reluctantly, go to bed, defeated and tearful, the heroine of a story I'd written without understanding it, a story that didn't make sense and that I didn't know how to rewrite.

*I*f you're someone like me, and you fall asleep watching the National Geographic Channel, your dream looks something like this:

You are the child of royalty, but you'll never ascend the throne because, people tell you, you're a girl. You know better: if the little girls you see around you are what girls are supposed to be, you're something else — not a boy, perhaps, but certainly not a girl. But you get good enough at passing that eventually you marry your half-brother, just as everybody expects, and you bear him a daughter.

You watch the child grow from a clever, bright-eyed infant to a bright graceful little girl who looks and acts a lot like you: she has your buck teeth and your imperious manner, both inherited from your dad the king, both as useless to her as they are to you. Meanwhile, your husband has gotten sick of old, bossy, butch you, and has started spending most of his time with his other wife, the young one with the straight teeth, and given her a son.

He dies of a heart attack in her bed. Tough titty, you think, but then you remember that now you're stuck with his little boy, the one who's just inherited your crown.

At the funeral, when nobody's looking, you grab a couple of objects from the pile of stuff that's going to get interred: his false beard, his favorite headdress. Alone in your bedchamber, you try them on, heart racing...

You start by administering the little prick's kingdom for him, the way a widow is supposed to. But as the months go by, you get bolder and bolder. You make your first appearance in public wearing the beard and headdress, and the crowd murmurs but doesn't rebel: you've gotten away with it! You start ordering statues and carvings of yourself as Hatchepsut, Pharaoh of Egypt. Your skin gets accustomed to the glue that holds the beard on, and you stop having headaches from the weight of the headdress.

Everyone gets good at concealing their surprise about what a fine Pharaoh you are, but you always knew you would be. Other Pharaohs, though, have been allowed to fuck up, make a bad decision, let down their guard. You don't dare; you can't just be a Pharaoh, or even a good Pharaoh; you have to be a perfect Pharaoh if you expect to go on living.

At a banquet, someone drinks a little too much and boasts about how if he could bend you over and have his way with you, you'd know your place. His friends shush him, casting nervous looks at you, but you ignore him. You go back to your royal bedchamber, send away all your assistants, and cry.

You are surrounded by many young men who want to do you favors, perform tasks for you, become part of your court. Senenmut's dialect places him as a commoner, but he's bright and witty and there's some kind of knowledge behind his eyes that makes you look at him first. The other courtiers hate him; behind his back, they call him "her," and make gestures with the index finger of their right hand penetrating their left fist, and snicker. But you give him a small task to do, commissioning a statue, perhaps; you think he might have nice taste in art.

The statue is beautiful, and you give Senenmut more to do. You make him tutor to your daughter, trusting him to teach her what girls need to know but also the things that nobody thinks girls need to know. You make him the architect of your temple. You spend almost all your available time with him; only he can make you laugh, can penetrate that icy loneliness at your heart. You both know that people think he's your lover — you saw the graffiti that showed the two of you fucking, and didn't know whether to laugh or to cry. The two of you had tried that once, but it didn't make either of you happy, and you never tried it again, and it didn't matter.

He is, in the end, the thing any leader needs: a competent, understanding and loving wife. And he is the one who holds your hand as the toothache turns into agonizing pain all over your body, and the pain turns to numbness, and the numbness to death.

*I*t had been hot for weeks in the way Sacramento gets hot, heat that seeps into the walls so that you can't touch your own home, heat that robs you of will, heat that presses you downward like a greasy thumb. It was long past bedtime. I lay naked, immobilized by the weight of the heat, on a bare, sodden cotton sheet. All the other bedclothes lay in a tangle at the foot of the bed. Frank lay as far away as possible, snoring hoarsely. I drowsed.

It was still night when I awakened fully and immediately: the curtains were blowing into the room, fluttering like bats in the darkness, and there was a rumble; it must have been the rumble that woke me. And I was suddenly, ecstatically cool. And rain pattered and then pelted and I lay in the darkness and breathed it all in, Frank asleep beside me. I don't know how long it lasted but I don't think it was very long.

After the rain quieted, I got up softly so as not to wake him, and went to the bathroom to look at myself in the mirror — that's how sure I was that something about me had changed, some sort of miraculous cellular reorganization. Maybe I was blond now, or thin, or tall; maybe my eyes were wiser; maybe I was a horse, or a supernova, or a man. But the mirror showed the same heavy-lidded, slightly protuberant brown eyes and the same wispy brown hair and the same plump feminine shoulders it always had.

Something had changed, though, something secret and numinous. Some sort of joy or wisdom had entered me for the first time through the open, wet window, entered through my closed eyes and at the center of my chest and between my sweating legs. Maybe the space had opened up with the rain, or maybe it had always been there, waiting for the rain to find it.

family portrait taken not too long afterward shows Frank standing behind me, leaning on the back of my chair, his flyaway hair temporarily tamed, wearing the sportcoat he donned perhaps twice a year. Our sons, one stretching toward adolescence, one still a sturdy preschooler, lean against my legs. I am wearing a simple gray cowlnecked dress, tidy leather boots crossed at the ankles, a gold chain. My hair is less than an inch long and has been coaxed into rebellious spikes.

And that's why I love musicals: they're the art form of anyone who has ever lived a lie. Which is more artificial, Fred Astaire dancing on the ceiling, or me attempting the life of a suburban wife and mother?

Inside the trim cashmere, I was bursting, uncontainable. And that's what a musical is: it's the moment when the emotion is just too much to contain, too much to express in words or actions, and the only thing you can do is, well, burst into song.

I cheated, of course. Like generations of married people before me and generations yet to come, I tried to reason it out: perhaps my desires were temporary, a craving that would vanish for good once sated; how could I know except to try? I waited as long as I could stand it, and then I did the only thing I could figure out how to do.

The first (but not the last) personal ad I answered turned out to be Marcel, a surly, scrawny little Frenchman who told me over coffee that my lipstick was too brown for my complexion but that he liked my shoes. It never occurred to me that this blithe assumption of the right to criticize my fashion choices might not bode well, because goddammit I was going to get to do real S/M at last.

I drifted dizzily through the next five days, learning that the idea of being too excited to eat was not, as I had always supposed, some peculiar sort of metaphor. (Of course I couldn't sleep or work either, but neither of those was anything out of the ordinary.) Some residual vestige of common sense made me tell my sympathetic friend Laura what motel I would be in and what to do if I wasn't back by 3:00.

I dressed in my best Macy's-dominatrix outfit, close-fitting black knit dress, black hose, high-heeled black slingbacks, notwithstanding that it was Sacramento in August and the temperatures had been soaring into three digits for days. My abused credit card was sweating too as I used it to check in. Marcel joined me a few minutes later in the room and we embraced humidly. Neither of us, we discovered, could figure out how to work the hotel air conditioner.

I ordered him out of his clothes — well, actually, I suggested that he take off his clothes — anyway, he took them off. We looked at each other for a long moment. I hadn't a clue what to do next.

Finally I sat in the desk chair and told him to lie across my lap. (This was the moment in which I discovered that the average female lap does not hold an entire adult male, even a very small French one; they're always falling off the edge of your knees.) I began to spank him, eliciting extremely satisfying little Gallic yelps and moans. I was so turned on I could hardly breathe.

After about twenty spanks he stood up rather suddenly and said, "OK, now let me show you what's *really* fun." A moment later he was stretched out flat on his back on the glistening polyester wall-to-wall. I was, he said, to walk on his supine body. I was to place my full weight on him but to try to keep most of it on the toes of my shoes so that my sharp heels didn't actually break his skin. He supposed that I could put my hand on the table for balance if I had to.

That was supposed to be really fun? Well, OK; I hadn't liked oysters the first time I tried them either. I stepped aboard, precariously. His penis immediately flew up to vertical like the flag on a mailbox.

Walking on a man feels like a rodeo event with no audience. Flesh slides over bone under your feet and you're constantly in danger of turning an ankle or falling ingloriously off. I felt myself growing dryer with every step, and developing a slight headache from the heat and the concentration. Marcel, however, was exultant and dripping. "There, doesn't that feel wonderful?!" he exclaimed. "Try putting your foot on my face."

Eventually he must have noticed that I wasn't matching his enthusiasm. "OK, let me show you the best part," he said. "Get off now." I dismounted, relieved and wondering what the best part was going to be, and he stood up. Then he placed his penis on the table. "Now stand on *that*," he said, helping me with his free hand to climb up. Figuring nothing could be more ignominious than what had happened so far, I placed my foot on his penis and pressed downward. This part *was* arguably the best, because the head of his penis as it bulged out of the shaft reminded me of one of those little rubber heads whose eyes and ears pop out when you squeeze them. Or maybe a cannoli, when you stick your fork in the middle and the cream blobs out the end. Or maybe...

"You don't like it?" he asked, crestfallen.

"Well, no, I'm not really getting much from it," I admitted.

He affected astonishment. His *last* girlfriend, he claimed, was so turned on by this that she'd been willing to step on bugs and rodents while he watched. At that point some long-suppressed fraction of my intelligence floated to the surface and I told him I had to leave.

I drove home, stopping on the way for a large Diet Coke and a package of Ho Hos, and called Laura to tell her that I was OK.

"How'd it go?" she asked.

"Um, not so good," I said. "Turns out what he really likes is for you to walk around on him."

"Oh," she said. There was a long pause while we both considered that.

"That sounds really boring," she said. And then we talked about something else. And I never saw Marcel again.

A knife proves and disproves edges.

Every knife starts as a blind shiny wall, rectangular and ordinary. It becomes a knife when it reaches outward, extends itself. It thins, it darkens; you feel it focusing, tightening, tapering, pulsing with purpose. Thin, thinner, down to nothing but a gleam. And that's where most knives end.

The perfect knife, sharper than sharp, would go on, though, thinner still, thin enough to see through, gossamer. And then it would be the ghost of a knife, part steel and part air, and then it would be all air and no knife, and nobody could say exactly where knife ended and air began. A knife like that could slide between atoms. A knife like that could convince you of the impossibility of knowing anything.

But knife is made for dividing. A knife convinces one thing that it's actually two. A knife does its work, and a stick of butter has become two cubes, each cube admiring its own reflection in the cooperative steel. Each cube is symmetrical and complacent. Each cube is invisible to the other. Each cube is unable to remember ever being any other shape.

How can the knife be both things, challenger of edges and creator of edges?

How can one device hold so much lonely potency?

*I*van's house had a thick, tangy, sexual smell that I'd never encountered before: a combination of stale pot, unwashed dishes and adult male bodies. Ivan proclaimed it "funky," and his English accent and actorish baritone gave the word the weight of truth.

I loved the smell from the moment I first inhaled it, dropping by in response to an ad looking for someone to write brochure copy for Ivan's acting classes. Frank's and my house didn't have much of a smell, and my nostrils were hungry for something stronger. I came back a time or two to take notes and edit drafts, and again, after the brochure was done, as often as I could — almost every day sometimes, while the kids were away at camp. Ivan's small, ropy-muscled body, clad only in red running shorts against the Sacramento summer heat, probably had something to do with it too.

I can't even remember what we did while I was hanging out there. Talked, I guess, and flirted, although the flirtations never came to anything. Ivan soon became my regular companion at the business events Frank hated; I could count on him to make witty conversation, and my female colleagues swooned over his plummy London accent, his long dark wavy hair, and his disproportionately large, veined, graceful hands. Everybody assumed he and I were sleeping together, and that suited me fine.

I was soaking up the smell at Ivan's one afternoon when his roommate John had a visitor. My favorite thing about Sharon from the beginning was her voice — oddly deep, with a funny wry drawl that rendered her observations even wittier than they already were. Her thick glasses minimized her eyes and gave her face an inhuman look, an impression that was accentuated by the dark flush that rose in her face midway through her third beer. Under her Levi's and polo shirt, though, her waist was narrow, her breasts large and firm.

The talk, as usual, turned to sex. She and John, it seemed, were occasional lovers, in spite of (or, perhaps, because of) John's longtime friendship with her ex-husband. Neither of them seemed in a hurry for a return engagement, though.

"My husband and I have talked about an open relationship, but he's not into it," I commented.

"Your — husband?" said Sharon, sounding startled.

"Yeah," I said. "I leave these low-lifes and go home to be a suburban wife and mom every evening. Why?"

"Oh," she said, blushing. "I thought you were a… lesbian."

Ivan laughed. "Yeah, everybody does. It's the hair." He affectionately rubbed my half-inch-long buzz-cut. I'd hoped that the eyeliner and earrings would turn it into a passably heterosexual fashion statement, but Sacramento wasn't a great town for subtleties.

I noticed Sharon's eyes lingering on me for several minutes afer that. When it was time for me to go home to start dinner, we exchanged phone numbers.

Two weeks later, I was facing her across a table with two empty beer glasses on it. It was late in the afternoon, after she got off work.

"No, never," I said. "Just men."

"Me, too," she said. "But I've always fantasized about a woman."

"I haven't, really. My fantasies are, um, equally inappropriate, but in a different way. Spanking, and such." We were both blushing madly.

"Maybe… we could combine them?" she said. I could feel arousal coming off her in waves, like heat.

*V*ita Sackville-West discovered women much earlier than I did, at nineteen — specifically, her childhood companion Rosamund Grosvenor, who had been brought over as a playmate to console six-year-old Vita when her father left for the South African war. By 1911, she writes, "we were inseparable, and moreover were living on terms of the greatest possible intimacy" — during a brief separation she wrote in a letter: "I do miss you, darling, and I want to feel your soft cool face coming out of that mass of pussy hair."

But Rosamund was just the training wheels for Vita's great passion with the exquisite Violet Trefusis, daughter of a King's mistress. I don't know that I approve of Violet: Nigel Nicholson, Vita's son and biographer, makes her sound narcissistic and needy. On the other hand, it would take a cold-blooded chronicler to pen a complimentary portrait of the woman who nearly destroyed his parents' marriage. Even Nigel, though, admits that Violet was "brilliantly gifted, richly subtle, loving everything that was beautiful.... a true rebel, conscious from an early age of the hypocrisy of the society in which she was brought up."

Vita and Violet's affair doesn't really interest me much — they seem to bring out the worst in each other in a lot of rather tedious ways. But then Vita meets a quiet young diplomat and finds herself enjoying his company in an entirely different way, and suddenly my interest rises. Harold Nicholson was, Vita wrote, "the only person of whom I think with consistent tenderness." A photo taken at the time shows a slender, graceful young man, with a neatly trimmed mustache over a rather feminine mouth. She recalled that Harold was "the best actual *playmate* I had ever known, and his exuberant youth combined with his brilliant cleverness attracted the rather saturnine me that scarcely understood the meaning of being young."

Vita went on to marry Harold. "He was like a sunny harbor to me," she wrote. "It was all open, frank, certain; and although I never knew the physical passion I had felt for Rosamund, I didn't really miss it." The couple went on to have three children, one stillborn. Together they created a home — Vita developed such tremendous horticultural skills that many biographical summaries list her as "an English poet, novelist and gardener" — and raised a family.

As Harold's work dragged him to the global hotspots of the day, and to trysts with many of the young men he encountered there, Vita tried to stay home to write, garden and raise her boys. Eventually, though, what she called her "wanderlust" would overwhelm her, and she would be off — sometimes masquerading as a working-class man named "Julian" — with Violet. Fueled by passion and rebellion, the two women dreamed of eloping together for good: Violet implored, "Be wicked, be brave, be drunk, be reckless, be dissolute, be despotic, be an anarchist, be a suffragette, be anything you like, but for pity's sake be it to the top of your bent.... Let's live, you and I, as none have ever lived before." Meanwhile, Harold suggested to Vita that Violet might like a volume of Sappho's poems for Christmas.

Harold was patient and almost unbelievably reasonable: "Why do you imagine that there is nothing between eloping with Violet and cooking my dinner? Oh what am I to do to win you back to calm and sanity? My love for you is certain, but yours for me sometimes seems so frail that it could snap."

But it did not snap. The fire died down, slowly, agonizingly. Vita wrote of the decade-long affair, "It was a madness of which I should never again be capable; a thing like that happens only once, and burns out the capacity for such a feeling" — a prophecy which turned out to be true. Harold and Vita both took lovers throughout their lives, mostly, but not exclusively, of their own genders; he called her affairs "your muddles," she called his "your fun."

Vita's other well-known connection, with Virginia Woolf, was of an entirely different kind: "One's love for Virginia is... a mental thing; a spiritual thing, if you like, an intellectual thing, and she inspires a feeling of tenderness... I have gone to bed with her (twice), but that's all." (This last sentence is both funny and moving; Marco Vassi would have loved it.) Notoriously, of course, Virginia went on to immortalize Vita's tempestuous androgyny in *Orlando*.

Vita and Harold were together until her death, and then he died a few years later. "We are sure of each other," wrote Vita, "in this odd, strange, detached, intimate, mystical relationship which we could never explain to any outside person."

I showed up at Sharon's house at the preappointed hour, early on a Sunday morning, to find her heavily hung over from the previous night's drinking. She wanted to go ahead anyway.

Since Marcel, I'd acquired a few skills. I spanked her soft wide bottom. I put clothespins on her tender nipples and took them off again, and put them on again, and took them off again, like a child with a toy. I had her crawl around the house, because I'd read somewhere that sadomasochists did that sort of thing — it made interesting red patterns on her knees and palms, but otherwise I couldn't really see the point.

I told her to go down on me and she did. I told her to stop, and she didn't.

Afterward, we lay side by side, flushed and sweaty, and she told me I'd discovered the cure for hangovers.

The marriage counselor asked, "If you could describe your ideal living space, what would it look like?"

Frank said, "A small house, quiet, with beautiful light in every room. Someplace where I could play the sax without disturbing anyone. Not much furniture. Not much stuff."

I said, "Maybe a loft in the city. Something big, where I could have parties. And where I could do S/M."

We looked at each other. We were living in a dim, sprawling, low-ceilinged ranch house in suburban Sacramento.

That Friday I had a meeting in Santa Rosa, and Frank had to go look at a project in Orinda. His whole family was meeting up in Santa Cruz for the weekend, and his mom was transporting the kids. I went to a mall, bought a cup of coffee and a book about divorce, and sat reading with tears streaming down my cheeks.

I left the book in the glove compartment and he found it there the next morning.

We went out for dinner and ended our marriage there, in Santa Cruz, a few miles from where we started it. No screaming, no recriminations, a few tears. We didn't even know the right way to get divorced, I guess.

*I*ve since been told that it's bad luck to give or receive a knife as a wedding present. If someone's foolhardy enough to send you one anyway, you're supposed to tape a penny to your thank-you note, which turns the gift into a purchase and lifts the curse.

But when I'd married into Frank's family, the one thing they'd understood about me was that I liked to cook. The pile of gifts scattered around our unvacuumed carpet had included six or seven cookbooks, a cutting board, an electric hand mixer, a yogurt maker, a Cuisinart, aprons, spoons, and several excellent high carbon steel kitchen knives. I still chop vegetables with those knives thirty-five years later. I didn't know about the penny trick, and I still can't decide whether or not we were cursed.

I'd noticed that married women kept one or two practical pillows on each side of the bed, but that single women had opulent mounds of them. I went to the variety store and loaded my cart with as many pillows as my credit card would allow. Then I paused, reconsidered, put a couple of the pillows back on the shelf, and added a set of snow-white sheets, the kind that an eczema sufferer can never sleep on without leaving little spots and smears of blood torn away in somnambulistic scratching.

Sharon's ex-husband had needed a brochure written for his business. I'd written the brochure in exchange for the bed that the two of them had occupied during their marriage and that had been dismembered in a garage since their divorce. It was a tarnished and dented old brass thing, but its corner posts were reinforced with rolled steel.

I thought for a moment and added a couple of hanks of rope to the pile.

Where is transcendence to be found?

What is the locus of that mysterious intensity that you know, deep in your bones, is somewhere, even if you've never seen it or felt it or really even heard it described?

Screaming with an open throat, raw-voiced, unstoppable. Sobbing like a lost child. Moaning, incoherent, delirious. Adrift in a sea of come, sweat, tears, juice.

Out of control. Out of control. Out of control. Repeat it again and again, until the words mean nothing, until all words mean nothing.

I didn't care, much, whether I made it happen for someone else or someone else made it happen for me: I just wanted it. Newly alone, directionless, contemplating my sad little pile of rope and hairbrush, ping-pong paddle and clothespins, I wanted it more than I'd ever wanted anything.

JACK'S SONG

In the center of a dark stage, a sudden spotlight reveals JACK. He is slender and dapper, reminiscent of Fred Astaire, or of Roy Scheider in All That Jazz. He is dressed in a natty tailored suit of immaculate pink satin with a matching pink satin derby. He leans on a slim cane glistening with rhinestones.

The music begins in syncopated 4/4 time, and the stage lights go up to reveal the CHORUS behind him: two round, hairy men, heavily bearded, dressed in wrestler's singlets. He begins to sing, lightly, smiling, moving to the rhythm.

JACK: I belong to a gal who is all I could desire
I'm her tool, I'm her pet, I'm the match that lights her fire.
So I'm opening my heart and I'm singing you this song
To acquaint you with the place where it's certain I belong.

JACK: Buh-buh-between her legs
CHORUS: It's a hairy situation
JACK: Buh-buh-between her legs
CHORUS: It's a wo-manifestation

JACK: I'm the Dick to her Jane, I am throbbing, hot and manful
I'm rebellious and ruddy and in fact, I'm quite a handful.
And whether I'm silicone, rubber or skin
The crowd that I want to belong to is "in."

JACK: Buh-buh-between her legs
CHORUS: That's the seat of my affection
JACK: Buh-buh-between her legs
CHORUS: That is my preferred de-rection.

JACK: Oh, my texture is firm and my figure cylindrical
           Sometimes I've a geyser, sometimes just a thin
           trickle.
           I am ready and willing, I'm as sturdy as a tree,
           In Ron Jeremy's dreams he's got someone
           like me.

JACK: Buh-buh-buh-between her legs
CHORUS: Never mind the right or wrong
JACK: Buh-buh-buh-between her legs
CHORUS: Just sing it:
CHORUS 1: Ding
CHORUS 2: Ding
JACK: Dong!

*Dance break — a whirling acrobatic tap number that concludes
with JACK standing on the broad shoulders of the CHORUS.
The tempo shifts and becomes slow and emphatic, and the
lights begin to dim.*

JACK (yearningly):
           I am stubborn and seductive,
           I am potent and persistent
           Underneath the flattest blanket
           I can make an awesome piss tent.
           For androgynes like her
           I am the optimal assistant
           But there's just one little problem…

The stage goes black.

JACK: I'm completely nonexistent.

Curtain.

III

FLYING

There is a knack to flying. Peter said all you had to do was think wonderful thoughts, but he lied.

It's easy enough to learn, though. A certain relocation of self to the center of the chest so that the shutters to the heart can be thrown open. A focal-plane trick of sharpening the present and blurring the past and future.

And then you rise up into the air, and fly.

Mischievous Peter never explained how you're supposed to get back down again.

*F*rank had moved out and the ranch house had a For Sale sign in the front yard. I walked into the kitchen to check on a pan of chicken drumsticks that were baking for dinner that night and for the kids' lunches the rest of the week.

As I came into the kitchen I looked across the pass-through and noticed a wasp flying around in the dining room.

I reached down to turn off the oven; when I stood back up, there were seven or eight wasps.

I bent over, took the chicken out of the oven and put it on the counter, and when I turned back, the dining room was full of wasps.

Heart pounding, I covered the chicken, stuck it in the refrigerator, and closed all the doors to the bedroom wing. I rousted the kids from their usual place in front of the TV and we tiptoed out the front door, feeling like refugees from a Hitchcock movie.

Several hours and some panicky phone calls later, I stood in the kitchen and surveyed the damage: a small wasp-hole in the dining room ceiling, a huge exterminator-hole in the hallway ceiling (the pest control guy had insisted he didn't need protective gear, and then he saw the ten-foot nest that had been forming evilly in the attic over the bedroom for years and years and turned tail and ran until he fell between the joists), bits of drywall in drifts like chunky snow over floors and rugs and furniture, and the whole thing blackened with a hairy, still-squirming layer of thousands and thousands of dead wasps. Suddenly I had a very clear vision of some malign deity looking down at me and cackling: *All right, bitch, you wanna be divorced? You're on your own now: deal with it.*

I asked Frank what we wanted to do about our pair of tickets to *Into the Woods,* the Sondheim musical about fairy tales. He said that we were not Noel-Cowardish enough to drive together into the city for a theater date just yet.

Fortunately, Russell's and my friendship had survived my clumsy collegiate seduction attempt, and we still saw each other from time to time when I had occasion to be in San Francisco. Russell had achieved one brief glimpse of paradise — leaving his law firm for a daily lunch hour with eight or nine trysts at the baths — before the viral window slammed shut, and, healthy but depressed, he had not ventured out since.

So it was Russell's blond head beside mine in the first balcony as we listened to Cinderella:

> *How do you know what you want*
> *Till you get what you want*
> *And you see if you like it?*

Frank's parents were milling with the other theatergoers in the lobby afterward, turning their shocked faces away from their recently-ex-daughter-in-law and her well-dressed escort. To this day, I can't think of a thing I could have said.

I had gotten what I wanted. It remained to be seen whether I'd like it.

ike most people, I am forked, more or less symmetrically: two legs, two arms, two eyes, two halves of the brain, two halves of the soul. There's the half that demands integrity, that loves its seamless skin and doesn't want it breached. Then there's the half that yearns for invasion, occupation, company. And right where they come together is my cunt.

My cunt is outer yet inner, private yet vociferous, armored yet vulnerable, part of me yet somehow separate. It is a burst baked potato, the place where containment fails and the overheated meat of me spills out for the tasting, complicated and discomfiting and fascinating.

Sharon, in spite of being as inexperienced as I, was an instantaneous cunt gourmet; her "soft cool face" never came out of my "mass of pussy hair." You may think this doesn't sound like a problem, but it was. I was discovering the "when do you stop?" issue that seems to saturate a great deal of sapphic sex (the male orgasm, while it lacks a certain something in repeatability, at least provides punctuation): as a result, I often found myself in the unenviable position of wishing I could watch TV instead of coming.

And then there was the reciprocation.

There are very few things I don't like to have in my mouth, and cunt tastes like several of the ones I do. Here, however, is the number of things I like to have jammed up against my face: none. Should you ever wind up having sex with me, please do not put your hand over my mouth. Do not hold my head when you're kissing me. Don't even *think* about gagging me, you pervert. And, most especially, do not ask me to shove my mouth deeply into what seems all too much like your internal organ.

While cocksucking is not on my top-ten list of ways to while away the time — well, let's face it, not even on the top-100 list — a cock is discernibly an appendage and not a giblet, and it is possible to suck cock without getting pubic hair up your nose. I suffer, it seems, from cunniclaustrophobia.

Sharon and I fought, made up, kissed, got drunk, fought some more. Starving, insatiable, she made me come, again and again. I turned over and tried not to notice the soft body trembling and sweating behind me.

For our one-month anniversary, she brought me a black silk scarf to bind her with, and a bottle of my favorite scent. For our one-year anniversary, she brought me a man.

Mike was a sweet enough guy, and he fulfilled his purpose of keeping my legs open to Sharon's busy mouth for a few more months. The three of us had sex in a summer meadow, in the front seat of Mike's '64 Lincoln, in the hot tub at the vacation cabin Sharon had rented for my thirty-fifth birthday, and in all three of our beds.

We were a triangle, stable and jolly as long as all of us were there, but any two of us receded into two-dimensionality. Mike and I devolved into joshing platonic buddyhood. Sharon and Mike bickered, flared, and stomped out of each other's lives. Sharon and I staggered along for many months in the miserable halting dance of one person who is in love and another who would like to be but isn't.

*F*red says that if he can't dance with Ginger, he just won't dance. But he's *gotta* dance — he's Fred, after all — so some cynical choreographer teams him with dozens of lithe blondes wearing bias-cut black satin and Ginger masks. Unbeknownst to Fred, the real Ginger hides teasingly behind one of them, and at the sound of her voice his dance becomes a double-take, then a floundering search, and finally a triumphant whirl.

Victoria-as-Victor enters the nightclub; black-clad dancers tango sensually across the stage. As they pivot, he, she, he sees that half are men wearing a woman's crimson pout masked onto the backs of their heads, and half are women rear-masked with tidy dark mustaches.

What if a gender-blind deity had danced Fred into that scene? Might Fred lift a flirty blonde mask to uncover the hopeful horse face of Edward Everett Horton? Would Fred say, as Victoria's lover did, "I don't care if you *are* a man"?

Probably not. I don't think he loved Ginger enough for that.

*S*haron left, but cunt stayed on my mind. The phrase "potential space," used to describe the closed-yet-open paradox of the vaginal vault, developed new echoes and resonances. I became fascinated with the rawness of cunt, tender as a partly healed wound, complex and multifoliate, tremulous and nervy. Even the softest epidermis — like, say, the skin of a penis — began to seem harsh and repudiating. I wanted in.

And, being the kind of girl I am, *in* is what I got. Imagine the months and years spooling by, signaled by a plump hand counting them finger by finger: first, experimentally, one; then, more confidently, two; then four — a long time stuck on four. Then, coached by a pale willing redhead whose thighs and calves formed an M in front of me (mentor, mother, muse) and who walked me patiently through the fussing and adjusting and several great dripping dollops of lubricant: the whole hand. Swallowed like a rabbit into a python. Surrounded. Massaged. Squeezed tight enough to grind dust off my metacarpals. And, oh my god, the steamy slippery volcanic heat, and the sounds she made, and the sounds *I* made.

It was several more years before I came while fisting somebody — a woman with whom I was, at the time, in love. I floated around moonily for a couple of weeks:

that's how profound our love is, that I can come just from putting my hand in her. Then, at a sex party, I was fooling around with another woman, a casual acquaintance, not coincidentally the mother of twins, and what I thought was going to be a little handjob turned into her cunt slurping up my arm like spaghetti. And I came. So much for *that* theory.

Now what I think is that cunts are so magical that they can transform one body part into another: a hand into a penis, presto — the power of the portal. If I were to paint a picture of a cunt, it wouldn't be a flower or a seashell: it would be a rosy version of the long vaulted emerald hallway down which Dorothy and her friends tiptoed, terrified and avid, confronting the unthinkable in search of the missing part.

Odysseus had to squeeze between Scylla and Charybdis. I wonder if he came when he made it through.

Next I discovered that cunts also have the power to turn the inanimate into the animate, Pinocchio's wetdream. Strap on an inert hunk of silicone and show it a cunt, and it suddenly wakes up, becomes richly innervated, wired into the brain and the spinal cord. There are, of course, logistical challenges — the woman who invents the target-seeking dildo and thus forever eliminates the awkwardness of "um, it fell out again" will become the century's most deserving millionairess — but I learned that every dildo harness is a potential Blue Fairy, turning its owner, should she desire it, into a Real Boy. I purchased several.

Of course, men have their own portals, located in roughly the same vicinity, and these have their own charm: puckered instead of slitted, with their complexities hidden inside rather than peeking out coyly, and with the added mud-puddle pleasure of forbidden earthiness. And I suppose that if nobody in the room has a cunt, this is the next best thing, and maybe someday I'll get as attached to assholes as I am to cunts, but so far I'm just not.

I do, however, like men. And since they don't have cunts, we use mine.

Which is how, after several decades of exuberant metasexuality, I have come to a renewed appreciation of penis-vagina intercourse. Now this simple animal pleasure seems like the most arcane of perversions: there he is, pumping and panting and sweating, thinking he's fucking a woman, seeing breasts and a cunt and an unquestionably female mega-butt, not knowing that the hand entwined and spasming in his hair used to be a cock and will be one again soon, not realizing that the nightstand full of silicone isn't a toybox but an organ donor.

And here's the thing: at the moment of orgasm it's not clear to me which of us has the cock and which the cunt. *We* are surrounded and engulfed; *we* are penetrated and invaded. We are through the looking glass, in a place where the most gender-specific of acts has blurred gender into meaninglessness. Now *that's* kinky.

That's the power of cunt. Cunt is the primal fissure. It dissembles and assembles; it transports and transforms; it bridges skin and entrail, orifice and protuberance. It does everything, in fact, but define.

Potential space, indeed.

*W*hen Amy came home with me as an eight-week-old puppy, she fit in my two hands, which made her a bit smaller than my surly middle-aged cat Happy (the least aptly named animal in the history of pethood). The cowering respect she learned that week stayed with her, even after she reached her full weight of well over 120 pounds. It didn't matter how blindly she was pursuing a thrown toy down the long hallway — if it landed within a six-foot radius of Happy, she would skid to a halt, drop to the floor, and whine pathetically until a greater power interceded to retrieve the object.

But she craved the old cat's approval — the approval of any cat, really. Perhaps, growing up with Happy as her only four-footed companion, she believed herself to be a cat. She played like a cat, and I never tired of laughing at the lumbering pathos of an enormous shaggy lab/poodle mix tossing a ball into the air and then batting it around the floor with her clumsy oversized paws.

By the time Happy was a senior cat, half-crippled with diabetes, he had mellowed enough that he occasionally allowed Amy to stretch out a foot or two away from him on the rug. During those brief détentes, Amy never closed her eyes; she didn't want to miss a minute. If I looked closely, I could see her quivering, just a little.

She grieved Happy's death, but never abandoned her passionate desire for feline companionship. We used to walk daily past a rose garden where lived a sleek, fearless calico that would occasionally deign to touch noses with her. On days when the cat was not out in the garden, the rest of the walk was a glum trudge.

And so it went, as Amy's muzzle grew grayer and her never-slim waistline thicker. Minnie, a six-toed tabby from the Oakland pound, tolerated Amy but never allowed the quivering black nose closer than a paw-swipe away. Amy would sigh, and stretch out as nearby as she was allowed.

The day came, the day I knew was coming, the day that Amy's faulty hips could no longer carry her big body up the stairs to her place by my side of the bed. The vet said, "While I'm on my way over, get her set up with her favorite thing, whatever it is."

I looked at Minnie, crouched across the room glaring. Sighing, I got out three pig ears instead, and arrayed them in front of Amy's front paws. Then I let the vet in.

Amy's tail was beating wildly at the sight of her favorite treat in triplicate; as she began to chew on the nearest one, the vet slipped the needle into her foreleg, and she lay her head down on a pig ear and died.

As I sobbed, Minnie got up and left the room, unmoved.

Sometimes, you settle for what you can get. Sometimes, that's enough.

"A drag queen trapped in the body of a woman" is how Dossie describes herself, and a casual glance into her closet confirms the self-diagnosis: the woman owns tiaras — not just one tiara, but multiple tiaras. Also: taffeta ball gowns, crinolines, corsets in a wide range of severities, leather skirts in lengths from crotch-baring to shoe-concealing, and enough thigh-high black nylon stockings to mask a platoon of armed robbers. At 65, she has had to abandon her beloved high heels, but she will undoubtedly spend the rest of her life wearing the hairstyle she calls "superannuated Shirley Temple" — a cropped tumble of ringlets in an alarming shade of orange.

When these curls fall down over her eyes, as they often do when her hands are tied behind her back, you need only squint a bit to see the Catholic schoolgirl who was regularly beaten by her father for asking the wrong questions, or the Bryn Mawr dropout headed for the East Village psychedelic revolution, or the battered, pregnant, homeless San Francisco flower child waiting in line for free yogurt handouts, or the young sex radical who raised her daughter with the love of her life and later held his hand as AIDS ate his mind and body.

During our years as friends and collaborators, Dossie and I have explored nearly all the cowboys-and-Indians possibilities of erotic roleplay: pirate and "proud beauty," sultan and harem slave, headmistress and new girl, warden and prisoner, and dozens more. In all of these, her costume — often a long white cotton nightie; sometimes a schoolgirl's pleated skirt; sometimes a corset over a decolleté silk blouse — is of paramount importance. I usually wear jeans and a tank top and then figure out a reason to blindfold her.

Something escaped, though, the night that we played prom queen and juvenile delinquent. For one thing, I'd finally found a role in which jeans and a tank top made sense. For another, with a switchblade (yes, a real one, although with a very dull edge) in my right hand and a fluttering pale throat in my left, I looked into her wide blue eyes, their pupils enormous with fear and arousal, and saw myself reflected: brown hair cut short and slicked back, mouth set in a thin sneer, eyes narrow.

I shoved her backwards onto the table and bound her in place. I was breathless and my cunt (encased in tight white Y-fronts) was slippery. Was I turned on because of the widespread thighs before me, framed in pink tulle? Or because of the cruel, aroused male stranger I'd seen, backwards and in miniature? Or both of them — two sides of a twisted coin?

I didn't know the answer to that question then, and I don't know it now. I do know, though, that those wide black pupils set in pale blue were the door to places I'd never have gone on my own.

*H*alloween, 1990. It's just after dark and the doorbell has almost stopped ringing.

The suit is secondhand, from Goodwill. Its previous owner was longer-legged and -armed than me, but the moment I saw it on the rack I loved the flat, formal gray wool with its winking thread of peach pinstripe, loved the gravitas it gave my middle-aged body when I tried it on, loved it even though I stood in a puddle of overlength pant leg and the sleeves hung past my fingertips.

I need the sleeves shortened on this jacket, I say. Is it marked? he asks. No, I say, I thought you could measure it on me. There is a short silence and the lines on his dark face deepen a little. All right, he says, put it on. How much will it cost? I ask. Thirty-five dollars, he says. But I only paid twenty-five dollars for the whole suit, I say. He says nothing. I sigh, slide my arms into the silk-lined sleeves, shrug the stiff collar up around my neck, hold out my wrist. Button the front up, he says.

Now the suit is hanging on the back of the closet, still bearing the aura of its previous owner — is that his aftershave I smell, or just a lingering whiff of my own shampoo? — but cleaned and altered and awaiting my occupancy.

I already own a lot of what I'll need. White oxford-cloth shirt, check. Necktie, check (well, stripe, actually, peach and charcoal). Black leather oxfords, check. Black leather belt with sedate steel buckle, check. White cotton knit briefs, check. Haircut, check.

The face is the tricky part. I peer critically into the bathroom mirror, assessing the brows I've been shaping since I was seventeen — back then every hair was an ordeal, but in thirty years the little nerves feeding the follicles have been numbed by my efforts, so that now tweezing is nearly painless and many of the hairs have given up altogether: I have a woman's eyebrows whether I want them or not. And a woman's cheeks, too, round and downy.

I frown at myself with my inadequate eyebrows, shake my head, let go of what can't be helped. First, everything off: I step out of my jeans and panties, peel off my t-shirt and bra, run a quick scan for vagrant dabs of toenail polish or fugitive specks of mascara. Turning, I face myself full-length, wearing only the gender signifiers I can't change: the round, mid-sized, slightly pendulous breasts that fed two children now grown; the scar across my lower belly from which those children entered the world; the large, dimpled, pale ass. This, like it or not, is what I have to work with.

Mustache or beard? asks the man in the theater store, friendly, collaborative, brusque. Beard, I say. Artificial hair, or yak hair? he says. What's the difference? I ask. Yak hair's better, but more expensive, he says, showing it to me. The hair is rough and curly, coarser than most real beards but it looks right. I turn it over and examine the crisp netting on the back. You use spirit gum, he says. You paint some on the back, then press it on your chin, then you take it off and let it dry until it's tacky. Then you have to put it on just right because it'll stick right away. And I can sell you some of this white stuff to paint into it, that way it'll match the gray in your hair. OK,

I say, the yak hair. And some spirit gum and the white stuff. Here, he says, you'll need this for taking the spirit gum off when you're done with it. Off my face? I ask. He hides his grin. No, use cold cream on your face, use this on the back of the beard and try not to get it into the hair. He puts everything into one little plastic bag, the size you'd use for a paperback book, and I shut it away in my purse.

I am aware of my breathing and the chill of the bathroom tile under my feet. I don't know where to begin.

Finally, I reach for the underwear, tighty-whities they call them. I am apparently the kind of man who wears tighty-whities, conservative, heterosexual, not very concerned with my physical appearance. The elastic comes up high at my waist, and the double layer of fabric pouches a little in front. Experimentally I slide two fingers into the opening. Hmm, you'd have to sort of hook your finger behind it and twist the whole thing and thread it out the hole, that seems like a lot of trouble, no wonder men just pull the waistband down and flop out over the top, I wonder why they still bother to build in these openings?

My hair hangs limp in eyebrow-length bangs. I push it back with both hands, study the expanse of smooth forehead, turn from side to side to examine the streaks of silver at my temples.

I scan the hair-treatment display at Walgreen's, mentally eliminating the bright-colored plastic packaging, the suggestive names ("Bed Head," "Totally Twisted," "Obey!"), anything pink or lavender or perfumed, until I find a squat round jar, blue glass with a metal lid, dusty and obsolescent. I twist off the lid and inhale the essence of 1962: train commuters with furled newspapers, ties knotted high in the morning and sagging loose by evening. Near it I find a small fine black Ace comb, the kind that fits in a man's back pocket.

How much? I start with an experimental quarter-sized daub, rub it between my palms, massage it into my hair. The comb sweeps my hair into a tidier arrangement, back from my face, but leaves it free to move when I shake my head no and reach for the jar. I add more and more again, until the comb leaves hard gleaming striations straight back from my forehead. I am a little dizzy from the scent of witch hazel, mineral oil, musk. The face looking back at me is not mine, exactly, but neither is it not-mine. I decide to ignore it for a while.

The white coloring for the beard comes in a little bottle with its own brush, like Liquid Paper. I've been paying attention for a few days to the gray in men's beards: it grows in stripes down either side of the chin, as though milk had dribbled out the sides of their mouths. Carefully I apply the paint, a couple of hairs at a time, comparing the result to the pepper-and-salt I see in the mirror. When I am finished the beard lies curled in my palm, striped like a little badger. I place it off to one side of the counter, away from my work area, but I keep glancing at it as I dress.

I had not considered the logistical problems inherent in breast-binding: I find I must grasp the end of the Ace bandage in my right armpit, lift my right breast with my right hand, pull the bandage taut across it, repeat the process with my left breast, then reach awkwardly behind myself to grab the dangling end and pull it tight across my back. Once I've completed the first two turns, though, the breasts are chastened, flattened firmly high on my ribcage, and I simply go on winding myself until I run out of bandage. The result looks unnervingly like an Elizabethan corset, but I shrug, figuring the solidly constructed suit jacket will hide any untoward bulges.

High thin black nylon socks — the elasticized band at the top is uncomfortably tight, and I know they will leave angry red indentations behind my knees. The pants have more fastenings than women's slacks, a little internal tab that buttons behind the zipper to hold the tummy flat, a hook and a button on the waistband, these would be hard pants to get out of in a hurry. The shirt, easy, I've been wearing men's shirts off and on for years, now whichever kind of shirt I wear it feels like the buttonholes are on the wrong side.

But my shirttails are out — oh, yes, I should have put on the shirt before the pants; it's been such a long time since I wore a tucked-in shirt. Still, I reason, one looks so silly in shirttails with one's bare knees gleaming over the top of one's socks, it's probably worth buttoning up your pants twice. I tuck in, rebutton, thread the belt through its loops. I sit on the toilet, lace on my oxfords, stand, note with approval the half-inch break of the trousers across the top of the shoe.

I turn up the shirt collar all the way around my neck.

Where's Dad? I ask, I bought this necktie and I don't know how to tie it. Your dad's busy, she says, but I can show you. You? I asked. Sure, she says, remember, I tied my own tie for the Maccabiah. Um, OK, I say. I look at the necktie loose in my hands and it looks altogether different, the way things look when you're seventeen and you thought you were doing something Marlene Dietrich-ish and cool and it turns out your mother did it a decade before you. Here, let me, she says.

I hitch the tie up close to my throat with that funny little wiggling jerk that men use, thread the narrow end through the label on the back, smooth it down my chest, fold my collar back down. In the mirror I look cherubic, a choirboy head on a stocky businessman's body.

I turn from the full-length mirror and lean across the countertop to solve the problem of my face. First the eyebrows: I sharpen a gray-brown pencil to a needle point and draw in the hairs one by one, sketching rapidly like charcoal on paper. I fill in where the eyebrows would have been if I'd left them alone, watching my features close off, thicken, become sterner and heavier.

The beaming face of Dr. Dean Edell greets me from the rack of reading glasses, all marked with their level of magnification: 125, 150, 175, all the way up to 300, but even the 125s are too strong for me to wear comfortably. But then I notice a few pairs that are plain glass with a small flat-topped round area, maybe an inch in diameter, bulging out into a magnification lens. One pair is large, roundish, tortoise-rimmed, the height of fashion a decade previous. The top of the frame touches my eyebrows.

The glasses conceal the near-invisible difference between the color of the eyebrow pencil and the color of my eyebrows. My face has morphed from choirboy to nerd: still beardless, but defined by the goofy oversized specs. I grin and stick out my tongue at myself.

I expect the spirit gum to smell like something — model airplane cement? — but it is nearly odorless. I dab it carefully on the netting backing, where it glistens. This is the can't-turn-back moment, unambiguous, undeniable. I lift the beard to my face and press it against my upper lip, cheeks, chin, the glue wet and sticky and a little itchy. When I take it away it pulls slightly.

While the gum dries I take a moment to focus on my breathing, trying to keep it deep and regular in spite of the unfamiliar pressure of the pants, higher on my waist than I normally wear them, the internal tab holding my belly taut. A final deep breath, all the way in, all the way out, look into my own eyes, nod to myself, it's time.

I position the beard carefully a half inch from my skin, then, when I have it exactly in place, press it to my face. The edges of the coarse netting are harsh but tolerable. Immediately, though, I am driven frantic by the curly mustache tickling my upper lip, so I grab a pair of nail scissors and clip it back to a tidy mouth-frame. The beard is a barrier, a sort of mask: my usual range of facial expressions is curtailed by the stiffness around my mouth and chin. I wasn't planning to talk much anyway.

The face in the mirror is now a masculine stranger, but an unkempt one. I pick up the scissors again and begin to snip, learning the craft of beard-trimming as I go: shorter near the skin, longer but even at the center, fairly square across the bottom to avoid the goatish look of the middle-aged slacker. Satisfied, I press again around the edges and smile carefully at myself. Everything stays in place.

The full-length mirror tells me I'm almost done, but the fabric hanging loose in the front of my briefs says otherwise. Briefly I consider the selection of silicone appliances in my nightstand, but the implications seem overwhelming and I falter, then give up.

All that remains, then, is the jacket, which I shrug on, like armor, like vestments. I button two buttons, leave the bottom one open as I've seen men do.

My father looks back at me from the mirror. Or, wait, not my father — too short, too wide. My ex-husband. Some part of each. And something else undefinable, some new entity, still vague around the edges, more an embryo than a person.

That entity steps out into the living room. The dog, confronted with a stranger in her own home, begins to bark — deep, threatening barks trailing to an uncertain whine. Jay looks up and his eyes go round and his mouth falls open.

And everything changes: not a lot, but a little.

A sort of a myth…

She was never like other girls, nor like boys. She did not like running or wrestling. Nor did she like dolls or frills, and she complained that the harsh fabrics of her dresses chafed her skin intolerably. She had a boy's curiosity about sex and a boy's love of building and making. She liked books, and her pens and paints, and animals. Her toy shelf held both a child's cookstove, pink as a nipple, and a child's building set, blue as the sky.

Still, she grew up into a woman more or less like any other woman. Her hymen kept men out until she found a woman with a scalpel to overcome it. She married and gave birth — although something in her apparently found itself unable to produce a woman: her children were boys. She accepted men between her legs with warmth and no sense of wrongness.

At the peak of her womanhood, though, she was accosted by a god. His touch set her afire, burning away her strength and sense. She labored to feed him, and knelt at his feet, feeding herself with him, feeling full and redeemed.

Like all gods, he was playful. He loved games in which she was the god and he the mortal. She found she was skilled at such games: imitating godhood suited her strangely. From time to time, though, he would tire of the game halfway through, and roar out with fury, and she would shrink and cower and cry.

"I cannot play this game with you," she told him at last. "I am too frightened."

"I am sorry," he said contritely. (When a god says he is sorry, be careful.) "What can I do?"

"I will be a man," she said. "Make me a warrior, who feels no fear. Call him Thomas." And that night, with a warrior's strength and the manhood of a warrior, Thomas imitated a god so well that at his moment of ecstasy, he felt himself immortal, and the god felt what it might be like to die, and loved the feeling.

"We will shear my hair in the style of a warrior," Thomas said, and the god wielded the scissors. "Can I pretend to die again now?" the god asked, and Thomas said, "Not tonight, I don't feel like it."

One day, Thomas told the god, "If you want to die, go do it. I am a warrior and do not have time for your stupid games any longer." The god wept but did not die.

"I can no longer feed you," said Thomas. "It is unbefitting a warrior. Go feed yourself." And the god raged, but Thomas was without fear.

"I am tired of you," said Thomas, for all the world like a god. "Leave. Go find yourself another worshipper." And the god did, but never a worshipper as devoted as Thomas had been when he was a woman.

Thomas lived a long life, and went on to have many adventures. He traveled the world and told the story of what it had felt like to be a woman, and what it felt like to be a man, and what it felt like to love a god. He met other gods but found them pallid and lacking in interest. He met women and men who thought he was a god, but he knew he was not. Eventually, he lost interest in the gods and their doings, and sat at home, boring his grandchildren with stories. He did not know whether to thank the god who had changed him, or curse the god for making it necessary for him to change.

And that is the story of how a woman became a man, and became, for a while, just a little bit like a god.

*H*er fans thought she was a gay man writing under a female pseudonym, because no woman could possibly write with such tenderness and strength about men loving other men. From my perspective half a century later, it might be that Mary Renault was the first creator of slash fiction. Instead of Kirk/Spock or Harry/Snape (or, um, Hook/Peter), though, she wrote Alexander/Hephaistion and Theseus/Pirithou, often in a tone of swooning fangirl infatuation: many gay men trace their first glimmerings of homoeroticism to *The End of the Wine* or *The Persian Boy.* Mary's own first glimmerings took place in her late teens, their subject the statues of beautiful Greek boys in Oxford's Ashmolean Museum.

When Mary met her lifelong love Julie Mullard in nursing school, they thought they had invented the games they played together (although they had the sense to keep them concealed from their teachers and fellow students). Throughout their half century as a couple, however, neither one claimed the label "lesbian."

Lesbian or no, the harshly post-Victorian climate of 1930s England drove Mary and Julie away. Mary won a prize of $150,000, a fortune at the time, for a minor book called *Return to Night,* and it was their escape both from nursing and from England: they bought property in South Africa, where they both lived until Mary's death. There, they could convene openly with the noisy campy men that Mary loved and Julie tolerated — a notoriously terrible actress herself, Mary loved theater and theater people and spent as much time as she could with them. Her crushes on gay men cost her both emotionally and financially, though: most of her stupendous cash prize was frittered away on investment houses in South Africa, co-owned with two men she adored... until somehow it turned out that she and Julie were doing all the work and contributing all the money.

I've never read before about a woman who wrestled as much with wardrobe as Mary did. In earliest childhood, she played cowboys-and-Indians by the hour and pined for a cowboy suit of her own. And throughout her biography, every tale of an honor bestowed, a political point made or a journalist received is preceded by hours of trying to solve the perennial question of what to wear: it seems as if that cowboy suit might have solved everything if only she'd been allowed to wear it all her life.

In spite of her love for Julie, Mary apparently never liked women very much. When a straight male fan wrote her to talk about their mutual admiration of the female form, she wrote back, "So you really think most women are beautiful? That must be nice. I wish I did." Although she relented a bit late in life when confronted with a new generation of liberated women, she noted that women of her own generation had "this terribly stunted look," and added, "I've never been a feminist, simply because all those years my inner persona occupied two sexes too indiscriminately to take part in a sex war."

She wasn't much help when it came to gay rights, either. In spite of her relationship with Julie and her obvious masculinity, those who looked to her for support in that struggle were shocked and disappointed: she opposed the whole concept of gayness as "sexual tribalism," believing that men and women should love as the urge took them, moving freely and fluidly back and forth along the spectrum of sexual choices. She once suggested that "all men should love someone of their own sex until just over twenty, when they should marry and raise a family. They should, however, return to their own sex in middle age."

It's a shame that Mary didn't outlive post-Stonewall identity politics so that she could enjoy the slipperiness of gender and orientation in the twenty-first century. On the other hand, I'm guessing that she would have found a way to distance herself from that, too — she spent her life figuring out perfectly good reasons not to fit into any category of gender, orientation or politics.

She'd probably have hated this book.

*D*ossie went to the tantra class first, and came back saying that I had to go too, that these people were onto something. Then again, Dossie is a lot more comfortable with the aging-hippie-Northern-California thing than I am.

Levana, the instructor, was an abundant woman with moist brown eyes and a nimbus of frizzy gray hair, wearing a batik caftan. She told us, "Tonight you'll have experiences over and over that feel like you're falling in love with someone — and you will be." *Yeah, right,* I thought.

I hated almost everything about the class: hated the music, women's voices invoking deities I don't believe in, honey-sweet tedium backed by sitars and tambourines; hated having to dance in dopey circles, right-foot-in-then-turn, like summer camp; hated, hated, *hated* being told I was a goddess, because I'm not, and I don't want to be.

But then I found myself facing another woman, a woman I'd met for the first time during introductions twenty minutes before. I put my right hand on her heart and she put her right hand on my heart, and we each placed our left hand over the other's, so I was pressing her hand into my chest, feeling it warm and solid between my breasts. We looked deeply into each other's eyes. Hers were browny-green, with little gold flecks in them, and in them I could see the reflection of mine, chocolate-brown, and together they made a new color somewhere in between, the color of a ripe olive. We breathed in unison, in, out out out, in, out out out, in... and then we came. Both of us. Simultaneously.

And I fell in love.

I can't remember that woman's name now, if I ever knew it.

I never learned to like the music or the dancing, and I don't think Levana and I ever appreciated each other much; apparently I am not in touch with my goddess-self, and apparently that's a problem in tantra. But I went back anyway. For a while there I was going every month or so, sometimes for an evening, sometimes for a day, once or twice for a whole weekend.

One Friday night, in a tall-windowed building in a grove of trees in rural California: Dossie and I sit crosslegged on the floor, a few feet apart, in a roomful of other women of all shapes and sizes. This is a beginner exercise, a warmup for a whole weekend of tantra: learn to coordinate the breath with the hip undulation and the rhythmic tightening of the pelvic muscles, the tantra equivalent of first position. I've done this a hundred times by now, so rather than listening to the music or to Levana, I'm listening to Dossie's breathing. On about the twentieth inhalation I hear a little catch in her breath and suddenly I know that we were connected.

Here's how we are connected: I have sprouted an imaginary penis, and it has snaked out away from me three feet to my right and gone straight up into Dossie. She begins to tremble, and so do I, the little energy tremors that tantra people call *krias*. Her breathing starts to stir her vocal cords and she is moaning, and so am I. And then she is suddenly in my lap and we are both bellowing, shrieking, slamming into each other with every undulation, eyes locked, breath in synch, each cell in our bodies having its own little orgasm all at once, out of control, and we can't hear anything over the pounding of the blood in our ears and our screams that build to a climax...

And then it's over, and we've fallen away from each other and we're lying on the floor panting and soaked with sweat, our legs still tangled together, and nobody else in the room will look at us. *You were completely abandoned,* their eyes say.

here are three ways to have a penis between your legs. You can fuck one. You can give birth to one. Or you can be born with one. Two and a half out of three, and that's about as far as I can go.

bandoned. What an odd word, with its overtones of puppies gone feral in parks, of worried glances passed between sister and brother as the dusk lengthens. A word of things broken: connections, deals, rules. Something you had that you lost. Or, more precisely, something that had *you*, that let you go. A lonely word. An unrestrained word. A word unaffected by gravity.

The building used to be the Women's Club; in its seventy or so years it has housed poetry readings, women's groups, community theater, same-sex ballroom dance classes, lectures. These days it's a dance center.

I signed up for the dance class because I'm feeling old, and some days everything hurts, and exercise seemed like it might help, and in five decades of steadfast and cherished physical laziness there has been exactly one kind of exercise I've ever actually liked: ecstatic dancing, the kind of thing where a lot of people pound on drums in a heart-rattling, contagious rhythm so that people like me can jump, flail, twirl, boogie, whip our heads back and forth to get dizzy, stomp our feet and grind our behinds and make loud noises. Given that I have not yet found a troupe of drummers who are willing to come to my home twice a week so I can get my aerobic on, I went looking for an alternative, and found this class.

But as I feared, it's goddess music again: the dance instructor pushes a button on the CD player and the women's voices start up, complete with tambourines. Trying to tune this out, I have no distraction from memories of a lifetime of exercise classes, all the times I've been the fattest, or the slowest, or the clumsiest. And not only that, but there are mirrors, a whole wall of them. I'm toward the back, twelve feet or so from the mirror, without my glasses, so all I can see of myself is an almost entirely circular shape with bare feet on the bottom and my dubious homemade haircut standing in unkempt spikes on the top.

We begin to move. The instructor, Sandy, has long honey-colored hair pulled back in a tidy band, and wears a girly little skirtlet over her leotard, and is of course the sort of person whose picture is next to "lithe" in the dictionary; I bet she has no trouble at all being called a goddess. I recognize some of her moves from yoga: a sort of a crane thing, some squats that I'd normally expect to lead into a downward dog, something definitely warrior-ish. And some of it has a martial arts flavor, with punching and kicking that I kind of enjoy: if you can't achieve grace, violence is a decent substitute.

But Sandy's palm is facing forward and somehow mine is facing backward, and I can't seem to coordinate the step-step-turn-PUNCH because my feet and hands have forgotten that they were ever introduced. I struggle to stay in the moment, I focus on my breath, I've sat in that tantra class for months learning this staying-in-the-moment-and-breathing stuff and I'm supposed to know how to do it. Instead I am grimacing wryly, the kind of expression you'd make if you tripped over a threshold when someone was watching, the kind of expression that's usually accompanied by a shrug. Except nobody *is* watching and the expression makes me feel even stupider.

So instead I watch Sandy, how her muscles slide smoothly under the skin of her shoulders, and I wonder if her toes point like that all by themselves when she lifts her foot. Probably. It's probably a reflex. The girly-toes reflex. Something that goddesses have.

"OK," she calls. "Follow your hand around the room." She shows us: her hand drifts up and forward, and she follows it with her eyes and then with the rest of her body, stepping forward in a graceful undulation, like someone trying to catch a very slow moth. I start moving my hand and my body goes with it, and there's no way to do this part wrong, and as I drift around the room, nothing exists but my hand, and it belongs entirely to me. Next, two hands, pressed palm to palm, keep a little strength in your biceps, she says, but otherwise just lead where your hands follow. My hands lead me down into a wiggly squat, up into a stretch, round and round, and I even skip a bit, like a four-year-old. I am released from the mirror and I begin to rise.

Leaping around, bellowing YEAH WOOHOO YEAH, whipping my whole upper body back and forth like a flag in a hurricane, face stretched into a huge open-mouthed grin, and occasionally I see another woman drift past but I don't care what she's doing as long as I can keep on moving, and then suddenly something grabs me in its teeth and tosses me around: hips grinding, shoulders swiveling, mouth howling, neck alive, arms extended, arms flying, arms fluttering, arms coming back to center, heel of hand to center of forehead, just a touch...

and I feel that familiar zizzing sensation beginning to zoom around my body as though all my veins were long rope fuses and think "oh shit I'm going to come right here in class and please god let me keep it at least slightly low-key," and then it explodes and I manage to just moan slightly and not giggle insanely or burst into tears the way I usually do, although I'd like to.

Nobody noticed. I don't think anybody noticed. I hope nobody noticed.

I find the floor again, and go home, and never go back.

And yet:

Dossie and I are in a public dungeon, a big ugly warehouse on a back street of Los Angeles. We're sort of the guests of honor — we've been teaching an S/M workshop in this space all day, and most of the people who attended it are out on the floor tying each other up or whipping each other — but we wish we could just go back to our hotel and watch pay-per-view. Each of us has been propositioned by at least three men since we arrived: Dossie is not interested in them because they're men, and I'm not interested in them because they're annoying. And although our teaching contract doesn't specifically say that we must attend this party, it would be extremely rude of us to blow it off, and at some point in each of our pasts we were well-brought-up young ladies.

So we're here. And we're exhausted, and everybody else here seems to be very very straight and not too interesting, and we figure the best way to avoid them is to play together — even these folks know better than to strike up a chat with two people in the middle of a scene. So we play, more from necessity than from desire: some flogging, some biting, putting on a flashy show. We're turned on — arousal is pretty much a reflex for us after more than a decade of this kind of thing

— but we're also trying not to be too obvious when we check our watches to see if we can leave yet.

And then Jim and Jim show up, unexpectedly: they'd said they might, but we didn't really think they'd set foot in an environment as hetero as this one. Now the evening holds a new kind of potential; suddenly my feet stop hurting and my face grows warm.

Jim is one of Dossie's oldest friends, slim and handsome and white-haired, with an assured manner and an impish grin; he has bypassed my usual suspicion of rich good-looking people by being witty and sweet and adorable. Jim, every bit as endearing, is twenty years younger, with the kind of excitable adam's-apple you only see on tall skinny dark-haired guys. We'd had brunch with them that morning and I'd watched them with fascination, the way their movements synched, the quiet smiles they exchanged when they thought nobody was looking.

I can't remember who makes the first suggestion or the first move, except that I'm sure it isn't me because everybody knows that if you say your wish out loud it never comes true. Here, however, is what I do remember:

Four heads, one sleek and white, one dark and spiky, one pumpkin-colored and curly, one brown-gray and soft. Two (flesh-and-blood) penises, four balls, four breasts, two cunts, eight nipples. A tangle of eight legs, some hairy and muscular, some creamy and smooth, rolling over and over, up onto a massage table, back down onto the floor again, up against a wall. Fists gripping, fingers pinching, toes curling, thighs trembling.

Someone grabbing my arms from behind, pinning them back while someone else does something sharp-sweet to my nipples and I yelp.

Someone looking into my flushed face and saying, wonderingly, "Wow, it's like boy energy, playful and hot."

Screams. Moans. Sobs. Giggles. Howls.

An audience gathering, watching quietly, eyes huge.

Sitting behind someone on a massage table, wrapping my legs around a strong pair of hips, grabbing tough pectoral muscles in my hands and squeezing with all my power, humping from behind, feeling my nonexistent penis quivering, hard, shiny, invading a hot open asshole.

The inside of my skull a warm white whirling buzz. Three faces as familiar as my own. Every inch of my skin as sensitive as a clit, a cock, an open wound. My mouth, stretched into a wide uncontrollable grin, or grimace, or black hole, trying to consume them all and hold them outside time, inside me.

Someone's hand on the back of my neck, stroking upward against my recently clipped buzz cut, caressing its bristly plush: a man's hand on a man's head.

Here's what else I remember: some part of me reawakening, stretching, soaring. Beyond arousal. Beyond self. Beyond gravity.

The "angry inch," the unhealed wound. The scar that runs down the middle, the scar where Hansel tried to bridge the gap and couldn't, the scar where he became Hedwig, neither man nor woman. (The scar where my sons were pulled from my belly.)

We all try to fly across the chasm. The origin of love, says Hedwig, is the yearning to regain what's been torn away. Our hand works busily between our legs like a tongue probing the hole of a pulled tooth. Our eye follows avidly the missing part, the round breast, the broad shoulder.

Many try to turn the hole into the whole with sex, where the cock and cunt become one. But there's always the moment when they come apart, when we lie sweating at the far edges of the bed, mourning the impossible.

Others try to cross over, leaving one behind to become other, abandoning testicles or ovaries to find wholeness.

One is a temporary answer, one permanent, and neither heals the raw original wound. Even the most ecstatic flight must end, and we land, on one side of the chasm or the other. All we can do is gather strength for our next attempt.

Once I decided I needed to shave my head: I wanted to find out what the world was like without hair between me and it.

So one night, Jay and I drove up to Dossie's house, where she was living with a woman who used to be a Zen priest and knew all about shaving heads. We ate big bloody steaks and gooey sweet ice cream sundaes, and then Jay did the part with the scissors, and Dossie did the part with the clippers, and the ex-priest did the part with the razor, and when it was all over my head was naked, there was nothing between me and you. The room swam around me and my vision went dark and then bright, and I laughed and laughed, and they laughed too, and the hair lay on the floor where I had abandoned it, where I had abandoned my hope for a certain kind of story, a certain outcome that I would not have as long as my scalp shone pink and bare and unbeautiful.

Jay found the shaved head entertaining for a few weeks, and then started hinting that he missed my hair, and then the hints were not hints any more and we had a big fight. It's probably too simplistic to call that the beginning of the end, but really: if I can't fly away and come back different, then I've chosen, I think, the wrong point of departure.

I often cut my own hair these days, always quite short because I don't have the patience to wait for it to get longer, and sometimes it looks great and sometimes it doesn't. I get bored with it from time to time and comb in a swath of purple, or bleach it impossibly white. Sometimes I go to a barbershop and ask for a man's haircut, because I love the clean snap of the big white sheet that gets tucked around my neck, the quiet buzz of the clippers, the smell of witch hazel and disinfectant.

And the reason I can do these things is that I know that I can survive any outcome: if all else fails I can always shave it all off again, and, clean and ugly and abandoned, become someone else, fly away and start over again, from the beginning.

Exit Music:

NEVERLAND

$\mathcal{W}$arm afternoon light, a small fireplace, hardwood floors clean in the middle and dusty in the corners. Shelves of books, dog toys scattered everywhere, plants on every surface, wind chimes trilling in the windows. Ikea furniture mixed with thrift-store finds and a couple of family heirlooms. Standard aging-liberal bungalow décor, really.

But: in the basement, several Hefty Bags, each marked with a strip of masking tape that says DRAG. In the converted garage on the first floor, a steamer trunk, dusty on top, full of S/M gear. On the main floor, my office, where I write the books that earn the money that pays for all this. Our bedroom is on the top floor.

There are days when my spouse sits in the bedroom all day, coming down only to pee and eat. On those days, I try to find some work that I can bring upstairs, so I can sit next to him and we can touch occasionally. He watches TV with the captions on so as not to distract me, or plays games on his laptop, or dozes lightly, pain cutting channels from his nose to the corners of his mouth.

Last summer, in the front yard: "I'd feel a lot better if I weren't so fat," I said, slapping my big thighs where they flattened out against the warm concrete step.

His back was to me; he was planting something. "Yeah... maybe if you got more exercise," he said. "And we should really be eating more fruits and vegetables."

When he turned around to get another bulb out of the bag, I had my head in my hands and the sniffles were audible. "Oh, honey," he said, and sat down beside me on the step and put his arm around me. "What's wrong?"

"You weren't supposed to *agree* with me." My voice quivered.

"Ohhhhh..." he said, pondering. We sat together in the sun while I tried to get myself under control. He hugged me. "I'm so sorry, honey," he said, sincerely. "I keep thinking of you as a big dyke, and to a big dyke that wouldn't matter. But I forgot: you're a big fag, and of *course* it matters."

How could I not love a man like that?

I can't call him my "husband." I had one of those, and I know what the word means: it means someone who sighs and looks away when you overdraw the checking account. The person who made a beautiful garden so that I could enjoy it through my office window, who cooks enormous unclassifiable crock-pot concoctions that we can't finish in a week, who reminds me to drink enough water and to take my B vitamins so I won't get too stressed — that's my wife. When our close friends inquire after his health, they ask how my wife's been feeling lately. To everyone else, though, he's my spouse. It's an odd, stiff, unwieldy word, but it's the only one I've got.

Edward is six feet tall and thin. Enormous blue-gray eyes, long face, soft chin — sometimes he looks like David Bowie and sometimes like Bugs Bunny. His hair is a wavy wheatfield that would be the envy of many men half his age; he gets frustrated with its unruliness and wants to buzz it all off, and I beg him not to — I love to put my hands in it and feel its moist, coarse curls. Sometimes people tell us that we look alike, and I suppose I can see it, something perhaps in the large slightly protruding eyes or the teeth that make our dentist roll his eyes and sigh in distress.

He has perky little breasts. These days I don't think they look all that unusual; a lot of middle-aged men have breasts. But he tells me that when he was younger they got him glared at in the gay clubs — maybe because Edward likes his breasts, likes to wear tight t-shirts with the sleeves and neck cut away and the fabric worn thin so that his upper body looks like a teenaged girl's. I like this too: I've recently been pondering ways to instantaneously break in some more t-shirts to make them as soft, fine and translucent as his old ones.

He has a beautiful voice, deep and precise and emotive as an old-time radio announcer; he says his high school drama teacher taught him to talk like that.

Some days he walks upright, at a pace not much slower than mine. Most days, though, he leans heavily on a stout wooden cane, and I have to look back every few paces and stop while he catches up. Occasionally I'll see him from a distance — slow-gaited, forward-leaning, thick-spectacled, wearing a cap tipped over his eyes and several layers of sweatshirts and jackets — and mistake him for an old man. And then I go up to him and he grins, or sometimes grimaces, and the illusion is broken and I am relieved: not yet.

What's wrong with him? Nobody knows. We are now on our third expensive and temperamental neurologist. The injuries to his spine and joints, we know about: those happened twenty-five years ago, when he stepped between a baby stroller and a drunk driver. They account for the arthritis and maybe some of the muscle pain. But they don't account for the agony that comes on suddenly — every time in a different spot — and drops him to his knees, or the twinges in his hands and feet that he says feel like electricity shooting off the ends of his fingers and toes, or the poor coordination that means I must fill out the lengthy questionnaires that the neurologists demand and then ignore. Our family doctor, a good friend, says that for now we'll call it "Edward's Disease."

Edward's Disease means that I get to do most of the breadwinning, which is fine with me. My last partner let me earn all the money, too, and he didn't have anybody's disease.

Edward's Disease also means that we use the bedroom mostly for watching TV and cuddling and sleeping. That's less fine, but, you know, I'm fifty years old and I've had a lot more sex than most people. I go flying off on an adventure when I feel the need, and he's here waiting for me when I get back, and that's enough.

We got married at the very end of 2005, at the Alameda County Courthouse. He wore a black suit I'd given him for Christmas. It fit perfectly and made him look sleek and urbane: definitely David Bowie. I saw him in it and immediately realized that what I'd planned to wear was frumpy and absurd. The bride is *supposed* to be the beautiful one, but I still ran out into the chaos of an after-Christmas sale and bought a new sweater and slacks to get married in.

The rings we exchanged are made of titanium, with a hammered finish. Of course, you can't hammer titanium — some jeweler painstakingly made a mold with a hammered texture, and poured the molten titanium into it. But they look like hammered titanium rings. I love them: they're strong, and beautiful, and not exactly what they appear to be.

Most of our neighbors think we're a nice ordinary middle-aged couple — they don't know, or don't care, or are too polite to speculate about, what it might mean when a guy wears a tight t-shirt that shows off his breasts, or when a woman cuts her hair short and walks with a heavy-heeled swagger.

A few neighbors — the lesbian and gay man two doors down who got married and had a baby together, the mixed-race pair of aging sixties radicals across the street — know a different truth about us.

I'm not sure which picture is right, or if either one is.

I do know, though, that every night we turn out the lights, and I roll on my side and curl up, and softly, in the dark, the fronts of his long thin thighs press up against the backs of my short wide ones, and I feel my muscles soften and warm, and my eyelids grow heavy, and we are home.

ABOUT THE AUTHOR

Janet W. Hardy is the author or co-author of eleven books about alternative sexualities, including the underground bestseller *The Ethical Slut*. A mother, author, educator, editor, publisher and showtune queen, she lives in Eugene, Oregon, with her spouse, two dogs, a cat and several chickens. Visit her website at *www.janetwhardy.com*.

OTHER BOOKS
BY JANET W. HARDY

The Ethical Slut: A Practical Guide to Polyamory, Open Relationships and Other Adventures (with Dossie Easton), Celestial Arts Books, 2009

The Toybag Guide to Canes and Caning, Greenery Press, 2007

Radical Ecstasy: S/M Journeys in Transcendence (with Dossie Easton), Greenery Press, 2005

Sex Disasters... And How to Survive Them (with Charles Moser, Ph.D., M.D.), Greenery Press, 2004

The New Topping Book (with Dossie Easton), Greenery Press, 2003

The New Bottoming Book (with Dossie Easton), Greenery Press, 2001

When Someone You Love Is Kinky (with Dossie Easton; as "Catherine A. Liszt"), Greenery Press, 2001

The Sexually Dominant Woman: A Workbook for Nervous Beginners (as "Lady Green"), Greenery Press, 1999

The Compleat Spanker (as "Lady Green"), Greenery Press, 1997

About the Publisher

Beyond Binary Books is a new imprint dedicated to publishing the best of literary fiction and nonfiction from the far edges of gender, orientation, sexuality, ethnicity, and any other boundaries it can discover. For more information, visit *www. beyondbinarybooks.com.*